T0330665

Place Marketing
and Temporality

Much city marketing and branding activity is future-oriented; aimed at achieving a forward-looking vision for places. The aim of this activity is to attract visitors, residents and/or inward investment, and focus on communicating attractive place attributes to create a differentiated spatial 'product' that will appeal to particular target audiences. In seeking to achieve this, place marketing campaigns have been criticized for emphasizing generic attributes, such as accessibility, infrastructure and a skilled workforce—which can serve to homogenize places which in reality are very different. However, a city's distinctive character is a consequence of its history and development over time, and this book analyses the role of these temporal dimensions in place marketing and branding. The book analyses how the past—both material (i.e. the historic built environment) and intangible (i.e. routines, practices and the 'character' of the populace)—is appropriated, in order to 'sell' the city into the future. It acknowledges the inherent selectivity involved and discusses the factors influencing what is remembered from the past—and equally importantly, what is forgotten. Adopting a range of theoretical approaches to understanding temporality in this context, the book will appeal to advanced students, academic researchers and reflexive place branding practitioners by introducing a 'temporal paradox' incorporating both fixity (the material and immaterial elements of the city's past) and fluidity (relating to the creation of the place product as a dynamic assemblage of individual elements and attributes aimed at particular target audiences).

Gary Warnaby is Professor of Retailing and Marketing, based in the Department of Marketing, International Business & Tourism and the Institute of Place Management at the Manchester Metropolitan University.

Routledge Focus on Business and Management

The fields of business and management have grown exponentially as areas of research and education. This growth presents challenges for readers trying to keep up with the latest important insights. *Routledge Focus on Business and Management* presents small books on big topics and how they intersect with the world of business.

Individually, each title in the series provides coverage of a key academic topic, whilst collectively, the series forms a comprehensive collection across the business disciplines.

Fostering Wisdom at Work
Jeff M. Allen

Artificial Intelligence, Business and Civilization
Our Fate Made in Machines
Andreas Kaplan

Power in Business Relationships
Dynamics, Strategies and Internationalisation
Dariusz Siemieniako, Maciej Mitręga, Hannu Makkonen and Gregor Pfajfar

Global Digital Technology Convergence
Driving Diffusion via Network Effects
Ewa Lechman and Adam Marszk

Place Marketing and Temporality
Gary Warnaby

For more information about this series, please visit: www.routledge.com/Routledge-Focus-on-Business-and-Management/book-series/FBM

Place Marketing and Temporality

Gary Warnaby

Routledge
Taylor & Francis Group

LONDON AND NEW YORK

First published 2024
by Routledge
4 Park Square, Milton Park, Abingdon, Oxon OX14 4RN

and by Routledge
605 Third Avenue, New York, NY 10158

Routledge is an imprint of the Taylor & Francis Group, an informa business

British Library Cataloguing-in-Publication Data
A catalogue record for this book is available from the British Library

ISBN: 978-1-032-68978-4 (hbk)
ISBN: 978-1-032-68983-8 (pbk)
ISBN: 978-1-032-68993-7 (ebk)

DOI: 10.4324/9781032689937

Typeset in Times New Roman
by KnowledgeWorks Global Ltd.

Contents

About the author

Gary Warnaby is Professor of Retailing and Marketing, based in the Department of Marketing, International Business & Tourism and the Institute of Place Management at the Manchester Metropolitan University. His research interests focus on the marketing of places and retailing. Results of this research have been published in a wide variety of academic journals in both the management, history, architecture and geography disciplines. He is co-author of *Relationship Marketing: A Consumer Experience Approach* and *Pop-up Retailing: Managerial and Strategic Perspectives,* and co-editor of *Rethinking Place Branding: Comprehensive Brand Development for Cities and Regions, Designing With Smell: Practices, Techniques and Challenges* and *A Research Agenda for Place Branding.*

Acknowledgements

Whilst my name is on the cover of this book, much of the original research which has informed this discussion of temporality and place marketing has been a collective effort over the last 15 years. I was fortunate in having great collaborators in these endeavours. Thanks go to Professor David Bennison, now retired, who did so much on our 'Hadrian's Wall' project, and Professor Richard Koeck, director of the Centre for Architecture and the Visual Arts at the University of Liverpool, with whom I wrote papers on digital technologies and advertising in urban space, which opened my eyes to the possibilities of this technology for the purposes of place marketing and branding.

Particular thanks are due to my main research 'partner-in-crime' for over 25 years, Professor Dominic Medway, with whom many of the ideas in this book were jointly developed. I want to take this opportunity to acknowledge his generosity in allowing me to develop these ideas—some of which have been published elsewhere in other forms, and in particular, others that have not seen the light of day until now in this book.

Various previous drafts of papers incorporating some of the ideas have benefitted greatly from comments by colleagues, and here special thanks go to Professor Tim Edensor and Dr Michael Sewell (who introduced me to the concept of the 'useable past').

I'd like to thank my "Luxembourg cultural consultants", Anna Warnaby and Gabriel Zasman for taking us to Belval one wet December afternoon. The results of this visit can be read and seen in the final chapter.

Finally, I'd like to pay tribute to the patience and forbearance of my wife, Jenny, to whom this book is dedicated.

1 Place and time

Introduction and outline

In his novel *Invisible Cities*—which can be read as a meditation on place, time and memory—Italo Calvino states that the city consists "of relationships between the measurements of its space and the events of its past" (1997[1972], p. 10). In Calvino's book, the merchant and explorer Marco Polo ostensibly describes to the emperor Kublai Khan the cities he has known, all of which incorporate remembered aspects of his home city: "Every time I describe a city, I am saying something about Venice" (ibid, p. 86). In this book, I analyse a similar interweaving of time and place, albeit in the context of the marketing and branding of cities, and also places at other spatial scales such as regions.

This discussion is timely. Over 20 years ago Crang and Tavlou noted that a recurring theme within the contemporary literature on spatiotemporal theory has been "the shift from a time-focused approach to a concern for space" (2001, p. 162). The burgeoning academic interest in place marketing from the 1990s (and since the turn of the millennium, increasingly in place *branding*) is arguably a manifestation of this more overtly spatial 'turn'—although it has been suggested scholars should better understand the role of 'place' within place marketing (Warnaby and Medway, 2013). To this end, more recent work has investigated the multifaceted nature of the place 'product' (e.g. Warnaby and Medway, 2013, 2015), and from a place branding perspective, place 'identity' (see Kavaratzis, 2004; Kavaratzis and Hatch, 2013, 2021), and the multiple associations created by place (see Zenker and Braun, 2017), thereby reflecting the 'kaleidoscopic' nature of places (Cheetham et al., 2018). However, in the place marketing and branding literatures, a deeper understanding of the role of *time* is less evident. Consequently, I suggest that, in addition to the inevitable focus on *spatiality*, place marketing scholars should also incorporate a concern for *temporality*. Indeed, Reynolds et al. (2023), while acknowledging its salience in this context, suggest that to date, the investigation of temporality in place branding has been somewhat tentative.

Given Huyssen's contention that "[a]s fundamentally contingent categories of historically rooted perception, time and space are always bound up with

DOI: 10.4324/9781032689937-1

each other in complex ways" (2003, p. 12), there is a need for more detailed exploration of these spatiotemporal interactions in the context of place marketing and branding. The aim of this book is to incorporate a more overt temporal dimension into the study of place marketing and branding—specifically in relation to how places are *represented* in these activities (termed here the 'representation work' of place marketing/branding professionals), and specifically to analyse the role of time in this representation work.

The remainder of this introductory chapter defines—and outlines the development of—place marketing and more recently, the increasing conceptualization of places as akin to corporate brands (Kavaratzis, 2005, 2009; Kavaratzis and Ashworth, 2008), which has resulted in the growth of research into place *branding*.

Chapter 2, *Representational selectivity and narration*, briefly outlines how temporal aspects can be used in visual means of place representation, with particular reference to logos, and also the potential of digital technologies to provide a more immersive experience of place which can incorporate both past and present. In doing this, I highlight the inherently selective nature of these processes. Here, I focus particularly on the concept of *assemblage*, whereby selected place attributes are commodified and subsequently curated to create a place 'product' aimed at a particular target audience—and indeed, the same place might be considered as constituting multiple products, each aimed at a different audience. As part of this process, attractive place narratives may be designed to appeal to the appropriate audience(s). The inherent temporal dimension of such narratives is explicated using Paul Ricoeur's (1984) notion of the 'threefold present'.

Chapter 3, *Memory and forgetting*, discusses the factors influencing the choice of attributes that are commodified to market or brand the place, with particular reference to what is remembered from the past in order to realize a future-oriented vision for the place. This discussion draws especially on Andreas Huyssen's (2003) description of the contemporary trend towards a 'culture of memory', which is manifested in 'memory discourses'. In the context of place marketing, such memory discourses may be selective, focusing on aspects of the past that portray the city, region or nation in a positive manner. Consequently, some aspects perceived as undesirable may be 'forgotten' in that they are glossed over or ignored completely in place representation activities, raising possible issues of exclusion and the potential for contested representations.

Chapter 4, *Fluidity and fixity*, discusses the role of material—and more intangible—heritage in place representation activities. The importance of the historic built environment to place marketing is readily acknowledged (especially for tourist destinations), yet another aspect of place character is its more intangible heritage which is evident in customs, routines and the character of the inhabitants etc. (which in turn may foster feelings of place attachment through lived experience). Both tangible and intangible heritage can be capitalized upon by those responsible for marketing and branding the place. This arguably introduces a temporal paradox, whereby in a marketing and branding context, places could be regarded as *fluid* (in that they are dynamic assemblages of different attributes that are created and/or curated to appeal to target users), but also as *fixed* (in that there is a place character or 'essence' that accretes over time and which could be a potent means of differentiating from its spatial competitors).

Chapter 5, *Instrumental and existential temporality*, considers the nature of time in this context, structured using Ali Madanipour's (2017) distinction between instrumental and phenomenological time. Here, instrumental time focuses on issues of accessibility and convenience (which are important tropes in place marketing messages), and phenomenological time refers to a more subjective sense of time, linked to personal lived experience and being 'in' place. Thus, the emphasis within place marketing messages on instrumental time could be regarded in terms of economically oriented attempts to valorize urban space through the use of time-contingent initiatives and imperatives. In contrast, phenomenological time acknowledges the importance of factors such as place attachment and the meaning(s) that places have for people, which will accrue over time and can be a very potent factor influencing place attractiveness.

Chapter 6, *Re-evaluating temporality in place marketing*, draws together the various themes discussed in the previous chapters. It highlights Michel Serres' notion of time *percolating* rather than flowing in a linear fashion (see Serres with Latour, 1995), acknowledging the juxtaposed and multiple temporal layers that can co-exist in place. The implications for the narratives created through place marketing's representation work are explored from a poststructural geography perspective, drawing in particular on Marcus Doel's notion of 'scrumpled geographies' (Doel, 1996, 1999), where the still-visible remnants of the past are described as 'disjointures', with terms such as 'folds', 'intervals' and 'joints' used to highlight different facets of interlaced (dis)continuities in space and time. The book concludes by identifying further avenues for research into place marketing and temporality, drawing on the concept of the 'useable past' (Sunstein, 1995).

Defining place marketing

Kavaratzis and Ashworth succinctly define place marketing as the "conscious attempt of governments to shape a specifically designed place identity and promote it to identified markets, whether internal or external" (2008, p. 151). This practice has a long history over many centuries (Ashworth and Voogd, 1994; Kavaratzis and Ashworth, 2008; Ward, 1994, 1998), and the development of place marketing will be discussed in the next section of this chapter.

Developing this definitional discussion, Warnaby et al. (2002) synthesize a range of previous definitions to identify three important characteristics of place marketing:

1 Place marketing is the responsibility not only of governments (as implied by Kavaratzis and Ashworth, 2008, above), but also of a range of public, private and voluntary sector actors who may collaborate in order to implement entrepreneurial activities to benefit a particular location. Stubbs and Warnaby (2015) identify a broad range of potential place stakeholders potentially involved in such activity, including (but not limited to) politicians, governmental organizations, promotional agencies, infrastructure and transport providers, cultural and sports organizations, businesses, academic organizations and also residents. These stakeholders constitute what van den Berg and Braun term the 'strategic network', that exists to develop 'organizing capacity' within the place, defined in terms of "the ability to enlist all the actors involved and, with their help, to generate new ideas and to develop and implement a policy designed to respond to fundamental developments and create conditions for sustainable development" (1999, p. 995). This is accomplished through activities and initiatives aimed at relevant target market segments, which link to the next characteristic.

2 Place marketing is concerned with ascertaining and meeting the needs and expectations of a range of users and potential users. Given the multifaceted nature of the place, users and potential users can be many and varied. Kotler et al. (1999) identify place marketing's target markets as consisting of: visitors (both tourists and business visitors); residents and employees (which could include particular target segments such as students, skilled workers—and even unskilled workers such as fruit pickers, to fill labour shortages at certain times of the year); business and industry (with particular emphasis on inward investment, although this also includes incentivizing 'local' business to further invest and/or not move elsewhere); and finally export markets (i.e. producing goods and services that other places, people and businesses are willing to purchase, and linking the image of place to this strong export performance, consistent with the marketing principle of the 'country-of-origin' effect—see Papadopoulos et al., 2018; Usunier, 2006). Different aspects of the place may thus be marketed to appeal to these various target audiences, which links to the last characteristic.

3 Place marketing involves the commodification of selected attributes in order to promote a positive image of the place as a holistic entity. Thus, individual attributes and/or facilities located within the place may be regarded as 'contributory elements' that can be assembled to create the 'nuclear' product constituting the place as a whole (Ashworth and Voogd, 1990). Developing this notion further, van den Berg and Braun (1999) identify three levels of (urban) place marketing, comprising: (1) individual goods and services that can be marketed as discrete attractions/facilities but can also be combined

to create; (2) clusters of related services that can be marketed to attract particular segments of place users and which may in turn coalesce to create an overall perception of; (3) the urban agglomeration as a whole, resonating with Ashworth and Voogd's notion of the 'nuclear product'. This process of commodification is discussed in more detail in the next chapter.

Stages in the development of place marketing

Kavaratzis and Ashworth note that the attempts of public administrations (and associated stakeholders comprising the 'strategic network') to attract capital and people (usually through attempts to differentiate from other places that are perceived as competitors) "is almost as old as government itself" (2008, p. 151). A secondary theme in the literature focuses on the historical development of place marketing activities, usually through case studies providing detailed analyses of the promotional activities of particular places (see for example, Lucarelli et al's, 2021, analysis of the promotion of the city of Stockholm throughout the twentieth century and Sewell's, 2024a, 2024b account of the marketing of Colchester over the centuries), or alternatively extensive discussions of particular place contexts (such as deindustrialization) that have motivated place marketing activities (see for example, Neill et al's, 1995 discussion of Belfast and Detroit). Synthesizing accounts of the historical development of place marketing activities remain quite rare, and of these accounts perhaps, the most extensive is Stephen Ward's (1998) *Selling Places: The Marketing and Promotion of Towns and Cities 1850–2000*, which details a thematic (and broadly chronological) developmental trajectory for place marketing, incorporating the following five contexts: *Selling the Frontier*; *Selling the Resort*; *Selling the Suburb*; *Selling the Industrial Town*; and *Selling the Post-Industrial City*. These contexts are briefly discussed below.

Selling the frontier

This context, Ward argues, marks the beginning of place selling in the modern sense (i.e. occurring through the printed word and mass media). This was a particular US phenomenon, closely associated with the development of railroads and the granting of land for disposal to settlers to create homesteads. Later, this place selling activity developed into the intense promotion of frontier towns and cities as trading and administrative foci for these agricultural areas. Such 'boosterist' activity—which extolled the virtues of the place to inspire local pride and attract settlement and investment (Abbott, 2005)—was undertaken by a range of local stakeholders, including "the local newspaper editors who used their columns to proclaim and reinforce a spirit of progress and enterprise" and local businessmen, who "vigorously promoted their towns, increasingly through collective bodies such as local Boards of Trade, Chambers of Commerce and Town Councils" (Ward, 1998, p. 22).

Selling the resort

This was, according to Ward, a singular UK and European manifestation of the US-type boosterism described above. The notion of the resort had its origins in the spa towns of the sixteenth and seventeenth centuries, with their focus on health. By the early eighteenth century in the UK, the larger spa towns such as Bath, Buxton and Harrogate were fashionable summer resorts for the upper classes. However, the second half of the nineteenth century saw the emergence of the *seaside* resort aimed at ordinary working people, who were able to visit as a consequence of improved mobility arising from the growing availability of cheaper mass transport (again linked to railways). With the seaside resort, there was a new emphasis on pleasure and entertainment, with promotional messages reflected in slogans (especially in Britain and the US), which sought to "suggest the essence of a place, its appeal and its main market" (ibid, p. 55), disseminated via posters and press advertising.

Selling the suburb

In the early twentieth century, 'selling the suburb' was also associated with the development of mass transit systems within towns and cities, enabling urban populations to engage in longer commutes to their workplaces from newly developed suburban residential areas. According to Ward, advertising was integral to the selling of suburbia, and this activity was developed in conjunction with housing developers and railways, along with financial services providers (such as building societies in the UK), to establish the concept of owner-occupancy financed by mortgages. Indeed, Ward notes that promotional messages sought to communicate "the idea of home as an emotional construct, imbued with idealized notions of family life and of relationships both to nature and a wider community" (ibid, p. 110).

Selling the industrial town

With 'selling the industrial town', the targets of place marketing/selling activities changed, Ward argues, from a mass popular market to a small number of potential industrial investors. This "inherently changed the terms of the relationship between buyer and seller of place" (ibid, p. 144); for example, through the routine offering of financial and other investments to incentivize (re)location to that particular destination. Indeed, the extent of this place marketing practice leads Ward to suggest that it was more akin to 'buying industries' rather than 'selling places'. He describes the selling of the industrial town as "a down-to-earth, matter-of-fact business", with a focus on "an accumulation of relevant and accurate facts" about the place (see also Barke and Harrop, 1994; Burgess, 1982; Warnaby, 2009). However, these facts were often "being deployed to construct a picture of place as the boosters and re-generators would have liked it to have been", rather than it actually was (ibid, p. 163). Promotional messages in this context were signalled through key words and slogans, often emphasizing the place as a key 'gateway' to, or a 'hub' or 'centre' of activity, with an appropriately skilled workforce to allow the industrial investor to succeed there.

Selling the post-industrial city

Ward's final place marketing context of 'selling the post-industrial city' was driven by structural changes in the late twentieth century global economy, as traditional industries declined and replacements needed to be found if towns and cities were to avoid terminal decline. Ward notes that:

> City advertising campaigns were merely the most visible parts of a wider process of regeneration, normally to encourage growth in service activi-ties. Common to all was the promotion of tourism, including the devel-opment or refurbishment of cultural attractions such as museums and art galleries, the boosting of business conventions and the hosting of major sporting or cultural events.
>
> (ibid, p. 186)

Thus, the focus of this (urban) place marketing activity arguably moved from promoting the city as a site of production to marketing it as a locus of consumption, and in so doing often had to combat entrenched negative per-ceptions about the place. It is this final context that arguably characterizes much contemporary place marketing activity, mindful of the imperative to project place distinctiveness, and also the need to manage possible tensions between the places' projected (possibly idealized) image and (often bitter) reality.

Developmental phases in place marketing

Kavaratzis and Ashworth (2008) draw on Ward's work in articulating their perspective on how place marketing has developed over time through three discrete phases (which they suggest differ in their general approach to-wards marketing as well as the level of refinement within each phase). Kavaratzis and Ashworth emphasize that these phases do not follow a strict timeline or involve geographical distinctiveness, but argue that progression from one phase to another "was more a result of growing understanding and experience of the application of marketing". They also stress that "each stage was not superseded by the next but rather coexisted so that at any one time a number of these stages could be found, often even in the same place" (ibid, p. 154).

Place promotion

Various of Ward's (1998) place marketing contexts (such as the *frontier*, the *resort* and the *industrial town*) are incorporated by Kavaratzis and Ashworth into their first phase—*The Stage of Place Promotion*. This was characterized by the boosterist emphasis on overt promotional activity, described by Ward and Gold in terms of "the conscious use of publicity and marketing to communicate selective images of specific geographical localities or areas to a target market" (1994, p. 2). Here, the focus is on the intensive use of marketing communications tools to promote the existing attributes of a place.

Planning instrument

The second phase identified by Kavaratzis and Ashworth—*The Stage of Planning Instrument*—links developments in marketing thought (including the 'broadening' of the marketing concept to include social and not-for-profit contexts) with changes in the priorities and preoccupations of planning professions. This, they argue, facilitated the acceptance of place marketing among public sector place managers, especially as places were perceived as being more overtly in competition with each other, resulting in more entrepreneurial modes of (urban) governance and economic development (see Harvey, 1989). With this more marketing-oriented approach, Boisen et al. suggest that place marketing should have a "substantial influence on the actual development of the place" (2018, p. 6). Thus, place marketing professionals can help guide the creation of new—and the assembly of specific configurations of—place attributes to appeal to specific market segments.

Corporate brand

The final developmental phase identified by Kavaratzis and Ashworth—which they date approximately to the beginning of the new millennium—is *The Stage of the Corporate Brand*. This, they argue, incorporates many of the more recent principles of corporate-level, rather than product-level, applications of marketing theory and practice (e.g. corporate image, corporate identity and corporate communications etc.). They highlight some similarities between corporate branding and place marketing:

> Both have multidisciplinary roots, both address multiple groups of stakeholders, both have a high level of intangibility and complexity, both need to take into account social responsibility, both deal with multiple identities and both need a long-term development. In these senses corporate level marketing does seem to offer a multitude of possibilities for implementing place marketing.
>
> (2008, p. 158)

These developments have implications for the marketing of places; notably the growth of the practice and academic discipline of place *branding*, which is discussed in the next section of this chapter.

Defining place branding

As mentioned above, over the last twenty years, the lexicon of this area of academic endeavour has developed from an emphasis on place marketing to place *branding*, whereby places are regarded as analogous to corporate brands. In his seminal book *Building Strong Brands*, Aaker (1996) defines a brand in terms of a multidimensional assortment of functional, emotional, rational and strategic elements that combine to create a set of associations relating to the entity in question in the minds of the public. Places can obviously be regarded as entities about which associations can be created in the minds of users and potential users. For example, even if one has never visited a particular place, one can still associate it with certain attributes and characteristics from how it has been represented in news media, in films and books, or from stories one has heard about it from family and friends who may have visited. New York makes one think of the 'city that never sleeps', as in the song 'New York, New York' popularized by Frank Sinatra (although originally the theme song for Martin Scorsese's film of the same name, sung by its star, Liza Minelli)—and indeed, 'the city that never sleeps' epithet has since been applied to numerous other global cities, in order to reflect their vitality and vibrancy. Similarly, Paris is often referred to as 'the city of love', especially—to introduce a temporal dimension—in the spring, as immortalized in song by Cole Porter with *I Love Paris* and Tony Osborne's *Springtime in Paris*.

Resonating with Aaker's emphasis on the importance of branding in creating associations with companies and/or their products, Boisen et al. (2018) note the consensus in the place branding literature that this refers to the creation of positive associations about a particular place. This is evident in an oft-cited definition of the place brand by Zenker and Braun, which states that:

> A place brand is a network of associations in the place consumer's mind based on the visual, verbal and behavioural expression of the place and its stakeholders. These associations differ in their influence within the network and in importance for the place consumer's attitude and behavior.
>
> (2017, p. 275)

The change in nomenclature from place marketing to place branding has, according to Boisen et al. (2018), led to some 'conceptual confusions' between the two terms (along with the associated notion of place *promotion*)—a situation exacerbated by the fact that many appear to use the terms interchangeably, so that to some extent they become synonyms. Consequently, there have been calls for 'tighter specification' of these concepts (Hankinson, 2015, p. 27).

Indeed, Hankinson notes that, notwithstanding the emergence of the domain of place branding "through a process of convergence" (ibid: 26)—for example, across disciplinary boundaries—older concepts such as place promotion (as associated with Kavaratzis and Ashworth's first developmental phase outlined above) still coexist with these newer concepts. Indeed, Boisen et al. state that conceptual confusion exists both *between* and *within* concepts, going on to state that "[s]ome scholars prefer to view place branding as an instrument of place marketing, whereas other scholars prefer to view place marketing as an instrument of place branding" (2018, p. 7).

To help clarify this conceptual minefield, Boisen et al. suggest that the key task of place *promotion* is to communicate place offerings (through coordinated promotion to identified broad target audiences), whereas place *marketing* seeks to manage supply and demand through specific product-market combinations (resonating with the notion of the assemblage of different permutations of place 'contributory elements') aimed at specific market segments. By contrast, the main task of place *branding* is to manage a place's reputation through the creation of a brand *identity* (i.e. how those responsible for the management of the place want it to be perceived amongst target groups), leading (hopefully) to an attractive brand *image* (i.e. how the place brand is actually perceived).

The importance of developing attractive place images is reinforced by Kavaratzis, who argues that place (and specifically, city) branding "centres on the creation of a favourable image or the change of a negative or indifferent image" (2007, p. 703). This emphasis on perceptions of the place in the minds of those people who constitute the target audience(s) for this activity (and how they may be influenced) is also highlighted by Kavaraztis and Ashworth, who argue that managing the place brand is essentially an attempt to influence those perceptions in a way "that is deemed favourable to the present circumstances and future needs of the place" (2005, p. 507)—thereby introducing an explicit temporal dimension into the discussion of (place) branding.

The importance of the temporal

The influence of temporality is a theme of the general branding literature, especially in relation to those brands (both product and corporate brands) that capitalize upon their longevity and heritage—which in turn influences how they are managed (see for example, Balmer, 2013; Balmer and Burghausen, 2015, 2019; Urde et al., 2007). Indeed, its heritage can become a distinctive brand asset which is difficult to imitate by competitors (Balmer, 2013), providing a basis for differentiation in addition to other benefits (see Ooi, 2002; Slater, 2001). In their consideration of heritage brands, Urde et al. (2007) note that while focusing on heritage means that brands are necessarily grounded in the past, corporate heritage brands must embrace three timeframes: the past, the present and the future. Such 'omni-temporality'—referring to "the synthetical conflation of the temporal strata of past, present and future into a *sui generis* temporal form that is qualitatively different from each stratum separately" (Burghausen, 2023, p. 130)—resonates with Paul Ricoeur's (1984) notion of the 'threefold present', which is explored in more detail in the next chapter.

In the particular context of place brands, Reynolds et al. identify omni-temporality "as an important and overlooked dimension of the place branding process" (2023, p. 8). The influence of omni-temporality, they argue, shapes "the construction of brand stakeholders' meanings, exchanges and experiences with the brand and each other" (ibid, p. 8), which will impact upon the processes of place marketing and branding (discussed in more detail in subsequent chapters). This will also influence place marketing and branding messages—in other words, the 'representation work' of place marketers, whereby place attributes (in isolation, or more likely, in combination) are used to create (and convey) a place identity which will be perceived positively by the targets of this activity, who will, in turn, develop positive associations with the place. The nature of this 'representation work' is discussed in the next chapter.

References

Aaker, D. A. (1996). *Building Strong Brands*. New York: The Free Press.

Abbott, C. (2005). Boosterism. In R. W. Caves (Ed.) *Encyclopedia of the City*. London and New York: Routledge, p. 30.

Ashworth, G. and Voogd, H. (1990). *Selling the City: Marketing Approaches in Public Sector Urban Planning*. London & New York: Belhaven Press.

Ashworth, G. and Voogd, H. (1994). Marketing and place promotion. In J. R. Gold and S. V. Ward (Eds.) *Place Promotion: The Use of Publicity and Marketing to Sell Towns and Regions*. Chichester: John Wiley & Sons, pp. 39–52.

Balmer, J. M. T. (2013). Corporate heritage, corporate heritage marketing, and total corporate heritage communications: What are they? What of them? *Corporate Communications: An International Journal*, 18(3): 290–326. http://dx.doi.org/10.1108/CCIJ-05-2013-0031

Balmer, J. M. T. and Burghausen, M. (2015). Explicating corporate heritage, corporate heritage brands and organisational heritage. *Journal of Brand Management*, 22(5): 364–384. https://link.springer.com/article/10.1057/bm.2015.26

Balmer, J. M. T. and Burghausen, M. (2019). Marketing, the past and corporate heritage. *Marketing Theory*, 19(2), 217–227. https://doi.org/10.1177/1470593118790636

Barke, M. and Harrop, K. (1994). Selling the industrial town: Identity, image and illusion. In J. R. Gold and S. V. Ward (Eds.) *Place Promotion: The Use of Publicity and Marketing to Sell Towns and Regions*. Chichester: John Wiley & Sons, pp. 93–114.

Burghausen, M. (2023). The presence of the omni-temporal: Theoretical foundations of (corporate) brand heritage design. *Journal of Brand Management*, 30: 129–143. http://dx.doi.org/10.1057/s41262-022-00302-9

Boisen, M., Terlouw, K., Groote, P. and Couwenberg, O. (2018). Reframing place promotion, place marketing, and place branding – *moving beyond conceptual confusion*. *Cities*, 80: 4–11. https://doi.org/10.1016/j.cities.2017.08.021

Burgess, J. A. (1982). Selling places: Environmental images for the executive. *Regional Studies*, 16(1): 1–17. https://www.tandfonline.com/action/showCitFormats? doi=10.1080/09595238200185471

Calvino, I. (1997 [1972]) *Invisible Cities* (trans. W. Weaver). London: Vintage.

Cheetham, F., McEachern, M. and Warnaby, G. (2018). A kaleidoscopic view of the territorialised consumption of place. *Marketing Theory*, 18(4): 473–492. https://doi. org/10.1177/1470593117724608

Crang, M. and Travlou, P. (2001). The city and topologies of memory. *Environment and Planning D: Society and Space*, 19: 161–177. https://doi.org/10.1068/d201t

Doel, M. A. (1996). A hundred thousand lines of flight: A machinic introduction to the nomad thought and scrumpled geography of Gilles Deleuze and Félix Guattari. *Environment and Planning D: Society and Space*, 14: 421–439. https://doi.org/10. 1068/d140421

Doel, M. A. (1999). *Poststructuralist Geographies: The Diabolical Art of Spatial Science*. Edinburgh: Edinburgh University Press.

Hankinson, G. (2015). Rethinking the place branding construct. In M. Kavaratzis, G. Warnaby and G. Ashworth (Eds.), *Rethinking Place Branding: Comprehensive Brand Development for Cities and Regions*. Cham: Springer Verlag, pp. 13–31.

Harvey, D. (1989) From managerialism to entrepreneurialism: The transformation of urban governance in late capitalism. *Geografiska Annaler*, 71B: 3–17. https://doi.or g/10.1080/04353684.1989.11879583

Huyssen, A. (2003). *Present Past: Urban Palimpsests and the Politics of Memory*. Stanford: Stanford University Press.

Kavaratzis, M. (2004). From city marketing to city branding: Towards a theoretical framework for developing city brands. *Place Branding*, 1(1): 58–73. http://dx.doi. org/10.1057/palgrave.pb.5990005

Kavaratzis, M. (2005). Place branding: A review of trends and conceptual models. *The Marketing Review*, 5: 329–342. http://dx.doi.org/10.1362/146934705775186854

Kavaratzis, M. (2007). City marketing: The past, the present and some unresolved issues. *Geography Compass*, 1(3): 695–712. http://dx.doi.org/10.1111/j.1749-8198. 2007.00034.x

Kavaratzis, M. (2009). Cities and their brands: Lessons from corporate branding. *Place Branding and Public Diplomacy*, 5(1): 26–37 http://dx.doi.org/10.1057/pb.2008.3

Kavaratzis, M. and Ashworth, G. (2005). City branding: An effective assertion of identity or a transitory marketing trick? *Tijdschrift voor Economische en Sociale Geografie*, 96(5): 506–514. http://dx.doi.org/10.1057/palgrave.pb.5990056

Kavaratzis, M. and Ashworth, G. J. (2008). Place marketing: How did we get here and where are we going? *Journal of Place Management and Development*, 1(2): 150–165. https://doi.org/10.1108/17538330810889989

Kavaratzis, M. and Hatch, M. J. (2013). The dynamics of place brands: An identity-based approach to place branding theory. *Marketing Theory*, 13(1): 69–86. https:// doi.org/10.1177/1470593112467268

Kavaratzis, M. and Hatch, M. J. (2021). The elusive destination brand and the ATLAS wheel of place brand management. *Journal of Travel Research*, 60(1): 3–15. https:// doi.org/10.1177/0047287519892323

Kotler, P., Asplund, C., Rein, I. and Haider, D. (1999). *Marketing Places Europe: Attracting Investments, Industries, Residents and Visitors to European Cities, Communities, Regions and Nations*. Harlow: Financial Times Prentice Hall.

Lucarelli, A., Cassinger, C. and Ågren, A. (2021) Continuity and discontinuity in the historical trajectory of the commercialising of cities: Storying Stockholm 1900-2000. *Business History*, 65(8): 1390–1416. DOI: 10.1080/00076791.2021.1979517

Madanipour, A. (2017). *Cities in Time: Temporary Urbanism and the Future of the City*. London: Bloomsbury Academic.

Neill, W. J. V., Fitzsimons, D. S. and Murtagh, B. (1995). *Reimaging the Pariah City: Urban Development in Belfast and Detroit*. Aldershot: Avebury.

Ooi, C. S.. (2002). Persuasive histories: Decentering, recentering and the emotional crafting of the past. *Journal of Organizational Change Management*, 15(6): 622–634. http://dx.doi.org/10.1108/09534810210449569

Papadopoulos, N., Cleveland, M., Bartikowski, B. and Yaprak, A. (2018). Of countries, places and product/brand place associations: An inventory of dispositions and issues relating to place image and its effects. *Journal of Product & Brand Management*, 27(7): 735–753. https://doi.org/10.1108/jpbm-09-2018-2035

Reynolds, L., Peattie, K., Koenig-Lewis, N. and Doering, H. (2023). There's a time and place: Navigating omni-temporality in the place branding process. *Journal of Business Research*, 170: 114308. http://dx.doi.org/10.1016/j.jbusres.2023.114308

Ricoeur, P. (1984). *Time and Narrative* Volume 1 (trans. K. McLaughlin and D. Pellauer). Chicago and London: The University of Chicago Press.

Serres, M. with Latour, B. (1995). *Conversations on Science, Culture and Time* (trans. R. Lapidus). Ann Arbor MI: University of Michigan Press.

Sewell, M. (2024a) The use of the civil wars in Colchester's tourist image. *Annals of Tourism Research Empirical Insights*, 5(1): 100120. https://doi.org/10.1016/j.annale.2024.100120

Sewell, M. (2024b) The impact of the British Civil Wars on the meanings and uses of the urban topography of Colchester in the long nineteenth century. *Urban History*, First View, 1–18. https://doi.org/10.1017/S0963926823000780

Slater, J. S. (2001). Collecting brand loyalty: A comparative analysis of how Coca-Cola and Hallmark use collecting behavior to enhance brand loyalty. *Advances in Consumer Research*, 28: 362–369.

Stubbs, J. and Warnaby, G. (2015). Working with stakeholders: Rethinking place branding from a practice perspective. In M. Kavaratzis, G. Warnaby and G. Ashworth (Eds.) *Rethinking Place Branding: Comprehensive Brand Development for Cities and Regions*. Cham: Springer Verlag, pp. 101.

Sunstein, C. R. (1995). The idea of a useable past. *Columbia Law Review*, 95: 601–608.

Urde, M., Greyser, S. A. and Balmer, J. M. T. (2007). Corporate brands with a heritage. *Journal of Brand Management*, 15(1): 4–19. https://doi.org/10.1057/palgrave.bm.2550106

Usunier, J. C. (2006). Relevance in business research: The case of country-of-origin research in marketing. *European Management Review*, 3(1): 60–73. https://doi.org/10.1057/palgrave.emr.1500049

Van den Berg, L. and Braun, E. (1999). Urban competitiveness, marketing and the need for organising capacity. *Urban Studies*, 36(5-6): 987–999. https://doi.org/10.1080/0042098993312

Ward, S. V. (1994). Time and place: Key themes in place promotion in the USA, Canada and Britain since 1870. In J. R. Gold and S. V. Ward (Eds.) *Place Promotion: The Use of Publicity and Marketing to Sell Towns and Regions*. Chichester: John Wiley & Sons, pp. 53–74.

Ward, S. V. (1998). *Selling Places: The Marketing and Promotion of Towns and Cities 1850-2000*. London: E & FN Spon.

Ward, S. V. and Gold, J. R. (1994). Introduction. In J. R. Gold and S. V. Ward (Eds.) *Place Promotion: The Use of Publicity and Marketing to Sell Towns and Regions*. Chichester: John Wiley & Sons, pp, pp. 1–17.

Warnaby, G. (2009). Changing representation of the industrial town: An analysis of official guides in Bury from 1925. *North West Geography*, 9(2): 1–9.

Warnaby, G., Bennison, D., Davies, B. J. and Hughes, H. (2002). Marketing UK towns and cities as shopping destinations. *Journal of Marketing Management*, 18(9/10): 877–904. http://dx.doi.org/10.1362/0267257012930402

Warnaby, G. and Medway, D. (2013). What about the 'place' in place marketing? *Marketing Theory*, 13(3): 345–363. https://doi.org/10.1177/1470593113492992

Warnaby, G. and Medway, D. (2015). Rethinking the place product from the perspective of the service-dominant logic of marketing. In M. Kavaratzis, G. Warnaby and G. Ashworth (Eds.) *Rethinking Place Branding: Comprehensive Brand Development for Cities and Regions*. Cham: Springer Verlag, pp. 33.

Zenker, S. and Braun, E. (2017). Questioning a "one size fits all" city brand: Developing a branded house strategy for place brand management. *Journal of Place Management and Development*, 10(3): 270–287. https://doi.org/10.1108/JPMD-04-2016-0018

2 Representational selectivity and narration

Introduction

The previous chapter highlighted the importance of the commodification of selected place attributes to communicate a positive place image. From a marketing perspective, this 'curation' of place attributes to formulate a product to be targeted at particular types of place users (e.g. tourists, inward investors, etc.) is implied by Boisen et al. in their description of place marketing as managing supply and demand through "the market-led development of attractive and distinctive *product-market combinations*". This could, in turn, potentially result in "a substantial influence on the actual development of the place" (2018, p. 6 Original emphasis). This is consistent with the theoretical move towards 'relational' places, which in Cresswell's words, "are never 'finished' but always 'becoming'" (2004, p. 35).

Often, the place attributes appropriated in this manner by place marketers and branders have a temporal dimension. This is because they hopefully convey something of a place's essence, perhaps arising through long association with the place (as is the case with the historic built environment—which may of course have influenced the nature of the place's development through the ages), and/or because they constitute some kind of natural or built environment landmark and thus regarded as 'iconic' in some way. Using its attributes in this way potentially differentiates the place from its rivals in the ever-intensifying competition for inward investment, tourists, residents etc., that has motivated much place marketing activity.

In this chapter, I begin by considering some of the ways in which historical elements are used to represent the essential nature of a place for the purposes of marketing and branding. This discussion focuses especially on logos (which are becoming such a ubiquitous aspect of place marketing and branding that it is often emphasized that place branding is not just about designing a new logo—see Ashworth and Kavaratzis, 2009) and the potential for newer digital technologies to convey more effectively the experience of being 'in-place'. The resulting place representations are—perhaps inevitably—always selective, as the kaleidoscopic and multifaceted nature of place could arguably

DOI: 10.4324/9781032689937-2

never be fully captured by such means (which generally oversimplify a very complex reality). Indeed, the inherent selectivity of the dimensions of place highlighted by those charged with the management of marketing and branding activities—as part of strategies to "reinvent the city, weaving 'place myths' which are designed to make the city attractive as a site for external investment (Hubbard, 1996, p. 28)—is an important theme in the place marketing literature. This selectivity—which can create both dominant and obscured place identities (see Boisen et al., 2011; Colomb and Kalandides, 2010)—is discussed in more detail later in this chapter, along with the potential implications for the development of coherent and consistent place marketing 'narratives'.

Apprehending temporality in visual place representations

The practice of place marketing and branding is, it has been argued, essentially visual. This is perhaps unsurprising given that, according to Porteous, "sight is the common sense, the dominant sensory mode". Porteous goes on to suggest that the visual sense "yields more than 80 per cent of our knowledge of the external world" (1990, p. 4). This ocular emphasis permeates the place marketing literature and is implicit in early definitions of the topic. Ward and Gold state that 'place promotion' involves "the conscious use of publicity and marketing to communicate selective *images* of specific geographical localities or areas to a target audience" (1994, p. 2 Emphasis added). In a particular urban context, Hubbard and Hall suggest that it is "perhaps best to consider the entrepreneurial city as an imaginary city, constituted through a plethora of images and representations" (1998, p. 7). Kotler et al. highlight the importance of the visual, noting that "[v]isual symbols have figured prominently in placemarketing [sic]" (1999, p. 171).

Nowhere is this ocular-centrism more evident than in the emphasis on the logo as a primary mode of place marketing/branding representation. Logos refer to graphic and typeface elements that can be incorporated into the graphic design used by an organization to identify itself or its products (Warnaby and Medway, 2010). From a semiotic perspective, Zakia and Nadin (1987) regard logos as part of the sign system an organization uses to communicate itself to both internal and external audiences. Henderson and Cote (1998) suggest that a 'good' logo should: (1) speed recognition of the company or brand; (2) create positive affective reactions (as these can transfer from the logo to the product/company); (3) evoke the same intended meaning across people in order to communicate a consistent, clear message that is difficult to misinterpret; and (4) create a sense of familiarity. These criteria apply equally in the context of place branding.

Various elements of the built and natural environment may be featured in logos. For example, the logo of Cumbria County Council in the UK (within which is located the Lake District National Park) is a celebration of the distinctive topography of the area with the word Cumbria in the shape of a mountain range, with its mirror image below, as if reflected in a lake. Similarly, the logo of Innsbruck Tourismus comprises a jagged line representing part of the Nordkette Mountains that surround the city, and the logo of Südtirol (South Tyrol) in Austria represents a panorama of the Dolomite Mountains (see Warnaby and Medway, 2010). Thus, places blessed with distinctive natural environment features will often feature these attributes in their logos as a means of differentiating from perceived spatial competitors.

But perhaps the most commonly used place element incorporated into logos is the built environment, and here the influence of temporality may be more keenly felt as the architecture frequently used for such purposes has historical associations. Thus, 'landmark' architecture closely associated with the place in question can be used as a form of synecdoche, defined by Lanham as "the substitution of part for whole, genus for species and vice versa" (1969, p. 97—see also Warnaby, 2015, for further discussion of this in a specific place branding context). Consequently, the Eiffel Tower (used in many logos of Paris-based organizations) becomes synonymous with Paris, and a representation of the Brandenburg Gate is integral to the logo of the '*be Berlin*' place marketing campaign (described in more detail by Colomb and Kalandides, 2010).

In such activities, the use of the term 'iconic' to refer to the—particularly architectural—place landmarks appropriated in this way becomes increasingly commonplace. Jones notes that:

> …[the] recent embrace of what has come to be known as 'iconic' architecture can be understood as a continuation of longstanding attempts to mobilize major building projects, first, to materialize wider discourses of major social change, and second, to generate surplus value from urban space.
>
> (2011, p. 115)

He goes on to state that such "attention-grabbing buildings" may "help create instantly recognizable 'brand images' for places" (ibid, p. 115). The importance of this visual emphasis is, according to Hospers, not lost on place marketers. Referring to such landmark architecture, Hospers states that it "is not enough for a city to have image carriers in the built environment—it is important that these are photographed, reproduced and distributed via the media" (2009, p. 228), going on to state that if a city "does not have imageable and scenic features, it will be a hard job for city managers to communicate it" (ibid, p. 230).

Some iconic structures may be more amenable than others to such marketing treatment because they are particularly photogenic. One example of this is the bridge, not least because the term 'bridging' has many positive connotations in terms of bringing people together, forging links, and, of course, reconciliation—all attractive tropes for place marketers and branders. Thus, bridges—both old and new—are integral to many logos of local public administrations and also place-specific organizations such as destination marketing agencies (see Warnaby and Medway, 2008). For example, arguably the most distinctive architectural feature in the former industrial town of Middlesbrough in the North East of England is the Transporter Bridge over the River Tees, built between 1910–1911, which has been appropriated as the town's logo, along with the slogan 'moving forward' (which is indicative of the future-oriented emphasis of much place marketing).

Moreover, bridges may also be fundamental to place *creation*, as is the case with the Öresund Bridge, which when completed in 2000, provided the first fixed road link between the Danish capital of Copenhagen and the Swedish city of Malmö, which helped give Öresund its status as a *Euregio* (or cross border region) within the European Union, in addition to providing a very potent regional symbol (see Hospers, 2006). As Löfgren argues:

> The bridge was built not only by engineers but also by event managers, media consultants, webmasters, place marketers and brand builders…This bridge project was densely inhabited by visions, dreams and expectations: there was so much that this bridge could do.
>
> (2004, p. 60)

The importance of such iconic structures—many of which are rooted in history—in providing a visual representation which can serve to differentiate a locale by drawing on the rich associations between structure and place, can be very real. Furthermore, when a structure, by virtue of its longevity, becomes part of local 'folklore', such as 'the Transporter' in Middlesbrough—which, moreover, has featured in many films and TV series set in the area—it becomes an even more potent symbol of local identity, which can be capitalized upon by marketers and branders.

Going back in time through digital technologies?

In recent years, there has been an increasing focus within the wider marketing discipline on the concept of experience and the experiential (see Tynan and McKechnie, 2009), and the question can be asked, "Is place marketing and branding any different?" This is particularly apposite given the view that place is 'a lived concept' (Cresswell and Hoskins, 2008, p. 394).

Indeed, being in a place is inevitably a multi-sensory experience, and the focus on the visual in place marketing and branding—whilst understandable given that, as Porteous (1990) states, we take in over three quarters of our knowledge of the external world through our eyes—may in turn be somewhat limiting. As Porteous goes on to argue: "Vision distances us from the landscape; it is easy to be disengaged. Such is not the case for other sensory modes" (1990, p. 5). Consequently, Medway (2015) advocates the use of a multisensory approach in place branding activities, arguing that the vast majority of current branding campaigns are ocular centric (although some might incorporate other senses, such as smell—see Henshaw et al., 2016), and a more holistic approach incorporating all five senses would better convey the true experience of being in a place. In the particular context of place *representation* for the purposes of marketing and branding, the resulting conundrum is articulated by Koeck and Warnaby:

> …an important question arises of how such complex and vaguely defined phenomena as places can be most effectively represented, particularly given recent technological developments, which have created the potential to move from a monodimensional (that is, focusing on a static image) to a multidimensional promotion of place; namely, a more overtly experiential depiction, which more effectively conveys the importance of emotional connection through engagement with urban narratives, and embodiment within particular space.
>
> (2015, p. 189)

If marketers seek to foster an emotional attachment to place among their target audiences, then this may potentially be achieved through a broader feeling of *embodiment* in place (by incorporating as many of the senses as possible). However, even greater emotional attachment might be achieved through combining this embodiment alongside engagement with the place's history and heritage. One way of achieving this could be through immersive technologies, such as augmented reality.

To illustrate this, Koeck and Warnaby (2015) suggest that the ability to geo-reference human data to traditional maps has been enabled—and in turn, has facilitated—new analytical techniques allowing new forms of spatial data visualization and contextualization. Urban landscapes can thus be understood as a system of infinite layers, and the use of Geographic Information Systems (GIS) capable of overlapping data onto maps in layers can offer visualization of new relationships (enabled through the provision of additional information about a place's history and other contextualizing aspects), stitched into a representation of space (such as a map). This can enable the user to move not only through space but also (virtually) through time, thereby amplifying users' perceptions of reality, their experiences and the possibilities offered by the 'real world'.

An example cited by Koeck and Warnaby is the *GhostCinema* mobile app. This app was produced as part of the *Cinematic Geographies of Battersea* research project (led by the universities of Cambridge, Liverpool and Edinburgh), which built a database of over 600 films that were partially or entirely shot in Battersea or were in some way emblematic of the area. The mobile app was developed to convey the convergence of geographic and historical material in accessible narrative and visual terms, with which users can engage and share (through a social media link) the discovery of lost local cinemas and movies shot in Battersea. The app thereby performs a dual role of enhancing an individual's appreciation (and understanding) of—and engagement with—Battersea, whilst also promoting the sharing of content (e.g. stories, memories, histories) about the place developed by many other individuals. This arguably engenders the construction of collective knowledge and understanding of a place and which may provide the basis for the development of place identities and related co-created branding outcomes.

As technologies develop, the potential for such 'augmented' and co-created place marketing activities will only increase, allowing a more comprehensive and holistic representation of place—both past and present. However, even with such technologies, the kaleidoscopic nature of place means that any attempt to represent the almost infinite permutations and possibilities that exist within cities, regions and nations, means that any attempts at representation will inevitably be reductive to a greater or lesser degree. Consequently, the choice of which aspects to incorporate (and thus, emphasize) within these representation activities is crucially important, and it is this inherent selectivity which is now discussed below.

Selectivity

Thirty years ago, Ward and Gold acknowledged the inherent selectivity of place marketing when defining place promotion as involving the communication of "selective images of specific geographical localities or areas" (1994, p. 2). This use of 'selective images' is particularly manifested in the choice of iconic symbols which, as mentioned above, readily lend themselves to visual representation. Thus, landmark architecture can be mobilized for place marketing and branding purposes. However, Butler and Dobraszczyk also highlight more phenomenological—and temporally-oriented—benefits that may accrue from this:

> …images of the city are a powerful means of attraction—they act as memorable lures in a highly competitive market of cities jostling for funds. But they can also work to install a renewed sense of wonder at what is already there, or to lure us into more difficult terrain, whether places or pasts.
>
> (2020, p. 19)

However, a longstanding criticism of place marketing is a perceived *lack* of distinctiveness in the way(s) in which places are represented, regardless of the intrinsic nature of the places themselves. Eisenschitz (2010) argues that many of the same marketing techniques (and indeed, message content) are commonly used across places that, in reality, are very different from each other. In terms of place marketing's 'representation work', this is evident in the widespread use of a collage approach, described by Gold as "perhaps the most distinctive feature of place promotional advertising" (1994, p. 22), and the same representational playbook has been identified in place marketing websites (see Warnaby, 2015). In sum, the place image collage is a representational technique that resonates with notions of 'assemblage'—defined in terms of the entity formed from the coming together of parts (Anderson, 2012), "whose properties emerge from the interactions between [those] parts" (Delanda, 2006, p. 5). However, this incorporation of multiple place attributes into one visual representation still nevertheless serves to reduce the place's complexity and richness—especially through, arguably, a potential conflation of its different temporal dimensions as different place attributes relating to various historical episodes in the place's history are juxtaposed together.

Discussing how the juxtaposition of different times could be regarded as an aspect of postmodernism, Crang and Travlou argue that viewing place through a postmodern lens "can be portrayed as pitting a geographical against an historical imagination", in that it "destroys historical narratives as chronology and sequence and promotes a depthless synchronic collage that juxtaposes past and present moments in a fragmented city" (2001, p. 163). Arguably, much of today's place marketing activity is created in the crucible of the postmodern mindset—a bricolage of temporal titbits melded together to create an attractive communicational narrative which bears only a loose relationship to the ordered realities of historical sequencing.

Anderson (2012) highlights that regarding place as assemblage is consistent with a move towards what have been termed 'relational' places. Implicitly acknowledging the inherent temporal considerations at play, he notes that "[t]he notion of (terrestrial) place has thus changed from one that is sedentary and stable to one that is open to conditionality and emergence" (ibid, p. 571). Places can, therefore, be regarded as inevitably 'provisional' because they are "constructed by people doing things, and in this sense are never 'finished' but are constantly being performed" (Cresswell, 2004, p. 37).

In a place marketing and branding context, Reynolds et al. (2023) have investigated how place stakeholders understand and navigate temporality when developing brand positioning strategies, in terms of their decisions relating to how their place is represented. Reynolds et al. identify two contrasting 'time orientations' to help place stakeholders (including marketing and branding professionals) navigate the diversity of meanings that are assigned to the past, present and future of a place—in other words, to address the issue of *omni-temporality*, mentioned at the end of the previous chapter. One orientation is described as the 'one-dimensional freeze-frame', which refers to a tight focus on a single period in place branding representation work. Such a strategy may be especially evident in places whose 'aesthetic materiality' is dominated by buildings of a particular time period. Reynolds et al. cite the example of the city of Bath in South West England, where the Georgian era identity (manifest throughout the city's built environment) has subsumed other periods, including its Roman origins.

The other orientation involves 'panning across time-frames', with a panoramic perspective across different historical periods, highlighting how the past is connected with the present and projected into the future, thereby emphasizing—and indeed, celebrating—the place's omni-temporality. This resonates with Paul Ricoeur's notion of a 'threefold present', where past, present and future connect, thereby "substituting for the notion of the present that of passing, of transition" (1984, pp. 8–9). Here, Ricoeur posits, memory and expectation appear as modalities of the present, and this, I argue, has implications for place marketing activities. In the specific context of city marketing, Warnaby and Medway suggest, "the place emerges as a text constantly rewritten by human actions", which "also relates to the activities through which the place is represented for marketing and branding purposes" (2013, p. 351). Here, both past and present place elements are mobilized in the service of creating an 'expectation' of what those marketing the place aspire it to be (often articulated as a place 'vision').

The choice between these orientations is, of course, a deliberate one, which will reflect how the past is regarded among—and the power relationships between—those individuals, organizations and groups comprising the 'strategic network' (van den Berg and Braun, 1999) of the place, which could lead to tension and even conflict. Reynolds et al. acknowledge this, stating that "[p]ositioning places in time is entwined with omissions, contradictions, complacency and inequalities" (2023, pp. 5–6), and these issues will be discussed in more detail in subsequent chapters.

Narration

If the representation work of place marketing is innately selective in terms of the place elements that are appropriated to achieve the marketing goals set, then perceived positive occurrences from the place's past and/or their associated material attributes (such as heritage features of the built environment) are often explicitly accentuated in marketing activities (Short, 1999), and in brand positioning—whether focusing on a particular time period or spanning different time periods (Reynolds et al., 2023).

An example of this temporally oriented approach to marketing that develops a particular *narrative* of the place in question is the *Historic Manchester Walking Guide*, produced in 2017 by the Heart of Manchester Business Improvement District (which exists to develop activities and promotional initiatives to improve the attractiveness of the city and encourage more visitors to its retail core). The guide "takes in a thousand years of history, and illustrates Manchester's elevation from a small town to a global player". Emphasizing the fact that "[i]n Manchester, history is everywhere—if you know where to look", the guide outlines a walk from King Street to the Cathedral, "passing buildings and landmarks you may well walk by, but whose stories you perhaps didn't fully appreciate until now". The commercial intent behind its production is evident in the introduction, which also illustrates the possible role of the past in promoting the present:

Alongside the walk are some handpicked shops, bars and restaurants that have their own historic tales—a flavour of the ever-present past in a city that sometimes feels all about the now. Which means that your hour, your afternoon, or even your evening in Manchester can be about more than the latest openings, eateries or fashions (no matter how delectably diverting they are). It can be about time spent discovering the bricks and mortar stories this city has to tell, old and new, from then and for now.

The guide's descriptions of the featured retailers highlight the history (including architectural details) of the buildings in which they are located, and often of the businesses themselves, as shown in examples of what the guide calls "shops with a story", below:

Belstaff—Belstaff is a brand steeped in British history, as its Manchester base has a similarly illustrious past. This is a building designed by Victorian architect Alfred Waterhouse, one of 27 he built for the Prudential Assurance Company. He used blood-red brick for all 27, and got the nickname Slaughterhouse Waterhouse as a result.

Hervia Bazaar—Hervia may be found in a landmark new-build, but it began life as a Royal Exchange boutique, before the IRA bomb put paid to its trade. Its fashionable owners spent the next 18 years running a clutch of Vivienne Westwood stores before opening this, their own luxury fashion boutique. Choose from over 60 high-end brands, for men and women.

Camper—This narrow slip of a shop, artfully filled with men's, women's and kids' shoes, is located on Acresfield—the site of Manchester's annual fair for over 400 years. And while the building it inhabits is modern, look up: its frontage is decorated with bees, the long standing symbol of the city.

Barton Arcade—A thing of tucked-away beauty, the Barton Arcade is sandwiched between Deansgate and St. Ann's Square—and thus easily overlooked. Persevere, though, for its glass domes, tiered balconies and intricate ironwork. Home today to Lunya, the handmade shoes of Jeffery-West and Pot Kettle Black, it's one of the best examples of a Victorian glass-topped arcade in the country.

The guide essentially describes a route through the retail core of Manchester city centre and could be regarded as a place marketing-oriented 'narrative' where connections between the various (in this case, retail) attributes of a place are outlined in a certain order to 'show off' the attributes of the place to the best effect. The *Historic Manchester Walking Guide* is an example in a place marketing context of Michel de Certeau's concept of the 'tour' as a means of conveying what he calls the 'spatial stories' of places. These 'spatial stories' "traverse and organize places...select and link them together...make sentences and itineraries out of them" (1984, p. 115). Thus, according to de Certeau, tours are descriptions of places "that are made for the most part in terms of operations" (ibid, p. 119)—in other words, emphasizing movement, where the experience of place occurs in a certain choreographed order of (selected) constituent attributes (see Warnaby et al., 2018, for more detail of de Certeau's concept of tours in the context of place marketing).

This ordering of the representation and presentation of place attributes could be a form of place marketing 'narrative'. In any narrative, there is a temporal dimension implicit in the fact that there is a certain sequencing involved, whereby at any point in the story (or in a spatial context, the 'tour'), there are both past and future actions. Returning to the notion of the threefold present, Ricoeur (1984, pp. 10–11) suggests that narration implies *memory* in relation to the past (i.e. recounting events that have happened and are happening), whilst prediction implies *expectation* in relation to the future (i.e. in terms of articulating 'things to come'). If, as Cresswell (2004) states, places are constantly being 'performed', then there is a sense of the past, present and future continually in play. Thus, the past can be mobilized in the service of creating an expectation of what those who are marketing the place aspire for it to be, perhaps articulated in a place 'vision', which is invariably future oriented—indeed, Kaefer (2021) describes place branding as a future-focused activity, and as about anticipating what comes next.

Inevitably, through their inherent selectivity mentioned previously, place marketing narratives relating to the development of a place are inevitably a simplification in the sense that there will never be enough time or space to tell the complete 'story'. Thus, some aspects of the place will be remembered and included in the narratives and other aspects will be neglected or ignored entirely as they do not fit within the 'official' place narrative. This is highlighted by Griffiths, below:

> Place marketing works by creating a selective relationship between (projected) image and (real) identity: in the process of reimaging a city, some aspects of its identity are ignored, denied or marginalised. For example, attention may be drawn to a city's industrial or mercantile heritage, while the practices of class exploitation and slavery that may have made this possible remain under a veil of silence. Strong local loyalties and civic pride may be highlighted, but not the traditions of trade union militancy or revolutionary politics. Great play may be made of a city's cultural diversity but not the systematic racial discrimination that in all probability accompanied it.
>
> (1998, p. 53)

Thus, memory of—and forgetting about—what has happened in the place throughout its past is an inevitable part of developing place marketing narratives, and I turn to this in the next chapter.

References

Anderson, J. (2012). Relational places: The surfed wave as assemblage and convergence. *Environment and Planning D: Society and Space*, 30: 570–587. http://dx.doi.org/10.1068/d17910

Ashworth, G. and Kavaratzis, M. (2009). Beyond the logo: Brand management for cities. *Journal of Brand Management*, 16(8): 520–531 http://dx.doi.org/10.1057/palgrave.bm.2550133

Boisen, M., Terlouw, K. and van Gorp, B. (2011). The selective nature of place branding and the layering of spatial identities. *Journal of Place Management and Development*, 4(2): 135–147. http://dx.doi.org/10.1108/17538331111153151

Boisen, M., Terlouw, K., Groote, P. and Couwenberg, O. (2018). Reframing place promotion, place marketing, and place branding – Moving beyond conceptual confusion. *Cities*, 80: 4–11. https://doi.org/10.1016/j.cities.2017.08.021

Butler, S. and Dobraszczyk, P. (2020). Introduction - Manchester: Seeing like a city. In P. Dobraszczyk and S. Butler (Eds.) *Manchester – Something Rich and Strange*. Manchester: Manchester University Press, pp. 1–23.

Colomb, C. and Kalandides, A. (2010). The 'be Berlin' campaign: Old wine in new bottles or innovative form of participatory place branding? In G. Ashworth and M. Kavaratzis (Eds.), *Towards Effective Place Brand Management: Branding European Cities and Regions*. Cheltenham: Edward Elgar, pp. 173–190.

Crang, M. and Travlou, P. (2001). The city and topologies of memory. *Environment and Planning D: Society and Space*, 19: 161–177. https://doi.org/10.1068/d201t

Cresswell, T. (2004). *Place: A Short Introduction*. Malden MA/Oxford/Victoria: Blackwell Publishing.

Cresswell, T. and Hoskins, G. (2008). Place, persistence, and practice: Evaluating historical significance at Angel Island, San Francisco, and Maxwell Street, Chicago. *Annals of the Association of American Geographers*, 98(2): 392–413. https://doi.org/10.1080/00045600701879409

de Certeau, M. (1984). *The Practice of Everyday Life* (trans. S. Rendall). Berkeley/Los Angeles/London: University of California Press.

Delanda, M. (2006). *A New Philosophy of Society: Assemblage Theory and Social Complexity*. London: Continuum Books.

Eisenschitz, A. (2010). Place marketing as politics: The limits of neoliberalism. In F. M. Go and F. Govers (Eds.) *International Place Branding Yearbook 2010: Place Branding in the New Age of Innovation*. Houndmills: Palgrave Macmillan, pp. 21–30.

Gold, J. R. (1994). Locating the message: Place promotion as image communication. In J. R. Gold and S. V. Ward (Eds.) *Place Promotion: The Use of Publicity and Marketing to Sell Towns and Regions*. Chichester: John Wiley & Sons, pp, pp. 19–37.

Griffiths, R. (1998). Making sameness: Place marketing and the new urban entrepreneurialism. In N. Oatley (Ed.) *Cities, Economic Competition and Urban Policy*. London: Paul Chapman Publishing, pp. 41–57.

Henderson, P. W. and Cote, J. A. (1998). Guidelines for selecting or modifying logos. *Journal of Marketing*, 62(2): 14–30. https://doi.org/10.1177/002224299806200202

Henshaw, V., Medway, D., Warnaby, G. and Perkins, C. (2016). Marketing the city of smells. *Marketing Theory*, 16(2): 153–170. https://doi.org/10.1177/1470593115619970

Hospers, G. J. (2006). Borders, bridges and branding: The transformation of the Øresund region into an imagined space. *European Planning Studies*, 14(8): 1015–1033 https://doi.org/10.1080/09654310600852340

Hospers, G. J. (2009). Lynch, Urry and city marketing: Taking advantage of the city as a built and graphic image. *Place Branding and Public Diplomacy*, 5(3): 226–233. http://dx.doi.org/10.1057/pb.2009.10

Hubbard, P. (1996). Re-imaging the city. The transformation of Birmingham's urban landscape. *Geography*, 81(1): 26–36.

Hubbard, P. and Hall, T. (1998). The entrepreneurial city and the 'new urban politics. In T. Hall and P. Hubbard (Eds.) *The Entrepreneurial City: Geographies of Politics, Regime and Representation*. Chichester: John Wiley & Sons, pp. 1–30.

Jones, P. (2011). *The Sociology of Architecture: Constructing Identities*. Liverpool: Liverpool University Press.

Kaefer, F. (2021). Place branding: The future. In F. Kaefer (Ed.) *An Insider's Guide to Place Branding: Shaping the Identity and Reputation of Cities, Regions and Countries*. Cham: Springer, pp. 43–47.

Koeck, R. and Warnaby, G. (2015). Digital chorographies: Conceptualising experiential representation and marketing of urban/architectural geographies. *Architectural Research Quarterly*, 19(2): 183–191. http://dx.doi.org/10.1017/S1359135515000202

Kotler, P., Asplund, C., Rein, I. and Haider, D. (1999). *Marketing Places Europe: Attracting Investments, Industries, Residents and Visitors to European Cities, Communities, Regions and Nations*. Harlow: Financial Times Prentice Hall.

Lanham, R. A. (1969). *A Handlist of Rhetorical Terms*. Berkeley: University of California Press.

Löfgren, O. (2004). Concrete nationalism? Bridge building in the new economy. *Focaal - European Journal of Anthropology*, 2004(43): 59–75. https://doi.org/10.3167/092012904782311489

Medway, D. (2015). Rethinking place branding and the 'other' senses. In M. Kavaratzis, G. Warnaby and G. J. Ashworth (Eds.) *Rethinking Place Branding: Comprehensive Brand Development for Cities and Regions*. Cham: Springer Verlag, pp. 191–209.

Porteous, J. D. (1990). *Landscapes of the Mind: Worlds of Sense and Metaphor*. Toronto: University of Toronto Press.

Reynolds, L., Peattie, K., Koenig-Lewis, N. and Doering, H. (2023). There's a time and place: Navigating omni-temporality in the place branding process. *Journal of Business Research*, 170: 114308. http://dx.doi.org/10.1016/j.jbusres.2023.114308

Ricoeur, P. (1984). *Time and Narrative, Volume 1* (trans. K. McLaughlin and D. Pellauer). Chicago and London: The University of Chicago Press.

Short, J. R. (1999). Urban imagineers: Boosterism and the representation of cities. In A. E. G. Jonas and D. Wilson (Eds.) *The Urban Growth Machine: Critical Perspectives Two Decades Later*. New York, NY: State University of New York Press, pp. 37–54.

Tynan, C. and McKechnie, S. (2009). Experience marketing: A review and reassessment. *Journal of Marketing Management*, 25(5–6): 501–517. https://doi.org/10.1362/026725709X461821

van den Berg, L. and Braun, E. (1999). Urban competitiveness, marketing and the need for organising capacity, *Urban Studies*, 36 (5–6): 987–999. https://doi.org/10.1080/0042098993312

Ward, S. V. and Gold, J. R. (1994). Introduction. In J. R. Gold and S. V. Ward (Eds.) *Place Promotion: The Use of Publicity and Marketing to Sell Towns and Regions*. Chichester: John Wiley & Sons, pp. 1–17.

Warnaby, G. (2015). Rethinking the visual communication of the place brand: A contemporary role for chorography. In M. Kavaratzis, G. Warnaby and G. J. Ashworth

(Eds.) *Rethinking Place Branding: Comprehensive Brand Development for Cities and Regions*. Cham: Springer Verlag, pp. 175–190.

Warnaby, G., Koeck, R. and Medway, D. (2018). Maps and Tours as metaphors for conceptualising urban place representation for Marketing/Branding purposes. In M. Kavaratzis, M. Giovanardi and M. Lichrou (Eds.) *Inclusive Place Branding: Critical Perspectives in Theory and Practice*. London and New York: Routledge, pp. 96–110.

Warnaby, G. and Medway, D. (2008). Bridges, place representation and place creation. *Area*, 40(4): 510–519. https://doi.org/10.1111/j.1475-4762.2008.00825.x

Warnaby, G. and Medway, D. (2010). Semiotics and place branding: The influence of the built and natural environment in city logos. In G. Ashworth and M. Kavaratzis (Eds.) *Towards Effective Place Brand Management: Branding European Cities and Regions*. Cheltenham: Edward Elgar, pp. 201–221.

Warnaby, G. and Medway, D. (2013). What about the 'place' in place marketing? *Marketing Theory*, 13(3): 345–363. https://doi.org/10.1177/1470593113492992

Zakia, R. D. and Nadin, M. (1987). Semiotics, advertising and marketing. *Journal of Consumer Marketing*, 4(2): 5–12. http://dx.doi.org/10.1108/eb008192a

3   Memory and forgetting

Introduction: The past in the urban present

Linking to the discussion of selectivity (and resonating with Ricoeur's, 1984, notion of the 'threefold present') discussed in the previous chapter, an important issue within place marketing representation work relates to what is remembered—and appropriated—from the past to communicate a future oriented 'vision' for the ongoing development of the place in question. In introducing this discussion, I draw upon Andreas Huyssen's notion of a 'culture of memory'; namely, "a turning towards the past that stands in stark contrast to the privileging of the future so characteristic of earlier decades of twentieth-century modernity" (2003, p. 11). This culture of memory is, Huyssen states, manifest in 'memory discourses', which he argues have pervaded contemporary cultural and political spheres.

Huyssen (2003) notes how individuals have engaged in obsessive self-musealization through the use of video recorders, memoir writing and confessional literature. In the intervening twenty years since Huyssen's book was published, these trends have become even more pervasive with the rise of social media and blogging, where people are able to record their own remembered versions and understandings of events in their lives. Such 'memory narratives' are also evident with regard to places, manifested in "the historicizing restoration of old urban centers, whole museum villages and landscapes, various national heritage and patrimony enterprises, the wave of new museum architecture that shows no signs of receding" (ibid, p. 14). Such heritage oriented developments in the urban built environment imply a formalized, planned strategy to differentiate the place through its history and to attract tourism visitors seeking to know more about—and also experience—the place's past through its material presence in the contemporary landscape. This is consistent with the underpinning of conventional classifications of heritage by notions of tangibility (see Ross et al., 2017). Indeed, Leask (2006) outlines the criteria and process for UNESCO World Heritage Site inscription, which emphasizes—both implicitly *and* explicitly—the physical properties of the locations in question.

However, most places are not so generously endowed with a materiality characterized as representing a masterpiece of human creative genius or being of

DOI: 10.4324/9781032689937-3

outstanding universal value (UNESCO, 2005). Instead, they necessarily rely on communicating their 'offer' through more mundane, prosaic material attributes—but which are nonetheless resonant with meaning relating to the place in question. One possible example of these more mundane attributes are 'ghost signs', which have been the subject of significant academic study (see Schutt et al., 2017) and popular attention (see for example, www.ghostsigns.co.uk/).

'Ghost signs' refer to outdoor advertising, particularly from the period 1930–1955, which has been hand-painted directly onto the walls of buildings, many of which have survived to the present day (Schutt et al., 2017). Figure 3.1 shows an example of a ghost sign in Manchester, UK. Whilst they are throwbacks to a bygone age, Schutt (2017) argues that ghost signs have found new lives through books of collected images (e.g. Roberts and Read, 2021; Stage, 1989) and—importantly in terms of their dissemination—online.

Figure 3.1 H. A. Howard & Sons Ltd ghost sign, Manchester. Photograph by the author.

Indeed, technological advances have made it easier to record and share images via social media platforms, as well as dedicated websites (e.g. www. hatads.org.uk/catalogue/ghostsigns.aspx) that are often specific to particular locales and act as a nostalgic temporal focus for the places in question. In October 2023, Historic England, a public body "that helps people care for, enjoy and celebrate England's spectacular historic environment" (Historic England, 2023) acknowledged their importance, arguing that ghost signs can tell us much about our collective architectural, cultural and social history. It thus encouraged members of the public to upload images and stories of ghost signs to create an interactive map of these faded fragments of our urban heritage (see https://historicengland.org.uk/whats-new/features/ghost-signs/). Such 'revenants' from the past (Warnaby and Medway, 2017), are also in evidence in other formats, such as the tiled shop entrance shown in Figure 3.2, of

Figure 3.2 Jas Smith & Sons ghost sign, Prestwich, Manchester.

a bar in Prestwich in Manchester, which indicates a former business located in the same premises which is now lost to history (but its traces have deliberately been kept by the current owners).

Schutt (2017) recognizes that such preservation-oriented representation work can serve to document these small, but evocative, historic place details relating to brands in urban space that would otherwise be missed and which could potentially contribute to the distinctiveness of a town or city (see also, Warnaby, 2019). This is particularly apposite if the brands in question have a link to the place in which their ghost signs are located (e.g. relating to businesses previously situated in the locale rather than national brands). The inherent power of ghost signs to evoke a sense of nostalgia (even if sometimes fabricated) is illustrated in an anecdote describing how locations depicting London in the 1930s were created for the film *The King's Speech*. For some external location shots, replicas of 1930s adverts were painted onto the walls of terraced housing, and after filming was finished, local residents "wanted to keep the Bovril ad the team painted on a wall, but it had to be removed with a water cannon" (Bedell, 2011, p. 7). Indeed, such is the appeal of these old hand-painted signs in urban space, modern brands have also used this form of advertising. Some brands appear to be reviving this medium in the contemporary urban landscape. In 2008, the US whiskey brand Jack Daniel's used stencils to replicate the brand's famous logo on walls in UK cities. The design was apparently artificially weathered to make the signs look older, in keeping with the brand's usual communicational approach, which emphasizes tradition and history and highlights 'authenticity' based on the brand's heritage (Ghostsigns, 2008).

While ghost signs are a benign element in the—primarily urban—landscape, other landscape elements commemorating events and/or individuals in the place's history may be much more contentious. For example, recent years have seen numerous examples of conflict over statues commemorating historic figures that have been accused of association with, for example, former oppressive political regimes (see for example, Frigerio, 2021), some of the darker aspects of colonialism, including slavery (see Burch-Brown, 2022; Drayton, 2019) and the US Confederacy (see Benjamin et al., 2020; Morgan, 2018), to the extent that many such commemorative statues have been removed. Indeed, in the UK, there has been guidance produced to help public bodies review contested statues and other forms of memorialization, such as place names (see Stephenson et al., n/d).

The extent of—and in some cases the violence associated with—contestation over the material forms by which certain aspects of a place's past are memorialized raises some difficult questions about what can—and what *should*—be celebrated in the place's past—including for the purposes of place marketing. Sadler (1993, p. 191) emphasizes that place marketing strategies are "both a social and political construction", consistent with the agendas of hegemonic groups. Thus, as mentioned at the end of the previous chapter, some aspects of the place's past may be especially highlighted while other aspects are downplayed or ignored (Griffiths, 1998). Short uses a metaphor of light and shadow to describe the resulting promotional discourses:

> The first [discourse] is the positive portrayal of a city; the city is presented in a flattering light to attract investors, promote "development", and influence local politics. But every bright light casts a shadow. The second discourse involves the identification of the shadow, the dark side that has to be contained, controlled or ignored.
>
> (1999, p. 40)

Thus, if certain aspects of a place's past are celebrated—including in place marketing representation work, which could as a consequence be construed as a form of 'memory discourse' (Huyssen, 2003)—then other aspects may, by contrast, be forgotten. Indeed, Huyssen notes that:

> The turn toward memory and the past comes with a great paradox. Ever more frequently, critics accuse this very contemporary memory culture of amnesia, anesthesia, or numbing. They chide its inability and unwillingness to remember, and they lament the cost of historical consciousness.
>
> (ibid, pp. 16-17)

Consequently, the contemporary "boom in memory" may be "inevitably accompanied by a boom in forgetting" (ibid, p. 17), which the inherent selectivity of place marketing representation work may further facilitate.

'Forgetting' in place marketing

Marcoux suggests that forgetting can be regarded as "the process of allowing certain things or details from the past to slip from memory in order to move forward", and that "[s]elective forgetting is a way to come to terms with the past" (2016, p. 952). This resonates in a place marketing context, given that— to reprise the earlier quote by Short (1999)—certain aspects of the place's history are regarded as 'the dark side' to be contained, controlled or ignored. Indeed, the place marketing imperative to give the most positive (and probably selective) impression of the place being promoted in the minds of target audiences means that the act of 'forgetting' can result in a conscious erasure of more undesirable historical aspects. The potential moral and ethical implications are obvious, and the possibility for both the content and process(es) of the narratives within place marketing representation work to be contested is very real, particularly where some groups may be adversely affected by conflicting interpretations of what is worth remembering and/or forgetting about a place (Clegg and Kornberger, 2010; Reynolds et al., 2023). Being written out of place narratives, therefore, has the same negative connotations as being written out of history more broadly. E. H. Carr, in his seminal discussion on the nature of history, notes that:

> Our picture has been preselected and predetermined for us, not so much by accident as by people who were consciously or unconsciously imbued with a particular view and thought the facts which supported that view worth preserving.
>
> (1961, p. 13)

Thus, as far as the development of place narratives for the purposes of marketing is concerned, there are parallels with the truism that 'history is written by the victors'. Indeed, Broudehoux describes place branding as a field where "dominant groups use spatial and visual strategies to impose their views" (2001, p. 272). This resonates with Sadler's (1993) view of place marketing strategies as social and political constructions, which in a place marketing context may avoid some aspects of the place's past because they are awkward, uncomfortable or difficult to confront in contemporary times. Examples might include urban histories, materialities (evident in the built environment, such as commemorative statues and street names), and memories of slavery or totalitarian rule. Including these aspects of a place's history in place marketing 'representation work' runs the risk of representing the places in question in a negative and unattractive way; or, if crassly promoted, a tasteless sensationalization of human misery for financial gain. Yet ignoring them could be construed as attempting a conscious and intended erasure or—even worse—a denial of such pasts, as discussed below with regards to the cities of Liverpool and Manchester and their respective roles in the transatlantic slave trade.

Manchester, Liverpool and slavery

The above discussion re-emphasizes how place marketing can become a highly political act (Sadler, 1993) and easily entangled in competing historical discourses around neo-colonialism, race and political oppression, etc. How places deal with this is a delicate balancing act of commemorating (and remembering to not forget) the past 'bad in place' as a means of highlighting current 'good in place', in order to 'move on'. An example of where this has been successfully achieved to some degree is arguably the historic ties between the city of Liverpool and the slave trade. Viewed as a "shameful" stain on the city's reputation and image (BBC, 2007), this difficult past is now confronted and addressed in the city's International Slavery Museum, which is now considered an important attraction:

> The International Slavery Museum highlights the international importance of slavery, both in a historic and contemporary context. Working

in partnership with other museums with a focus on freedom and enslavement, the museum provides opportunities for greater awareness and understanding of the legacy of slavery today... It is located in Liverpool's Albert Dock, at the centre of a World Heritage site and only yards away from the dry docks where 18th century slave trading ships were repaired and fitted out... National Museums Liverpool is ideally *placed* to elevate this subject onto an international stage.

(www.liverpoolmuseums.org.uk – emphasis added)

Whilst Liverpool could be said to have acknowledged its role in the slave trade, its urban neighbour in the north west of England, the city of Manchester, has arguably been more reticent in this regard. Dodge states that in the nineteenth century, Manchester was transformed into a major commercial city, funded in part through a worldwide trade in cotton goods:

> ...the requirement to import raw materials meant that Manchester was drawn into complex trading relations with distant places of production, and, along with Liverpool, bound into the responsibility for fostering slavery, a shameful history that still remains rarely acknowledged.
>
> (2020, pp. 113–114)

He goes on to state that Manchester "was built—and rebuilt—on the money that flowed from cotton, with whole streets and impressive commercial buildings serving the textile trade coming to symbolise its success" (ibid, p. 114). However, it has been argued that the concomitant links to the slave trade were until quite recently part of the city's 'dark side', and Bakare suggests that this is because of the city's remote relationships with the enslaved people who produced the cotton (when compared to Liverpool, where the docks were an unavoidable reminder of its role in the slave trade). He notes that:

> ...in Manchester, you can walk down Brazil Street or past the cotton bud fountain in St Ann's Square and have no idea of their links to chattel slavery. You can buy fashionable menswear and eat at a swanky restaurant in Manchester's Northern Quarter that both use the city's "Cottonopolis" nickname in their branding, completely untethered from its origins.
>
> Walking around Ancoats, a former textile district where cotton warehouses have been turned into luxury flats, there are no signs of the neighbourhood's connections to slavery. The city council has made no apology, and no study has been commissioned into how the profits of human suffering helped develop the world's first industrialised city.
>
> Today, some argue that contemporary Manchester has, like its pioneering industrialists, done a very good job at putting distance between itself and slavery.
>
> (2023, online)

Bakare states that it was hoped that the 200th anniversary of the abolition of slavery in 2007 would serve as a catalyst for some form of commemoration and remembrance and "the start of a recalibration of Manchester's history" (2023, online). Two years later, when the city-region's destination management organization, Marketing Manchester, launched a major branding campaign—titled 'Original Modern', highlighting Manchester's seminal role in the development of the modern industrial city and which built upon the history of the city to explain the 'essence of Manchester'—this element of the city's past was largely ignored (apart from a brief mention of 'cottonopolis' in an introductory piece to the brand document, written by historian and author Tristram Hunt).

The focus of historically oriented commemoration in the 'Original Modern' branding campaign was a series of place-based temporal narratives of a set of 'exemplars' (including individuals, institutions, organizations, buildings, and one of the city's football clubs). These exemplars were, in turn, linked to 'six key values' which Marketing Manchester associated with the 'Original Modern' city; namely, *Making a Contribution to the City*, followed by the imperatives to *Introduce a New Idea, Be Progressive, Challenge Convention, Think Global* and *Be Ambitious*. For each exemplar, the accompanying narrative reveals how from inception—and over time—it has typified some or all of those six values that contribute to the Original Modern concept. Most of the narratives relate to more recent individuals, groups and organizations, but for others, the longevity of their subjects is emphasized; for example, the co-operative movement starting in 1844 and Manchester United Football Club dating from 1878. One of these narratives relates to a former cotton mill, but in terms of its recent incarnation as a home to over 50 artist's studios, art gallery, recording studio and venue space.

Linking to Ricoeur's (1984) concept of the threefold present (mentioned in the previous chapter), this orientation towards the past in the 'Original Modern' brand positioning could be regarded as a 'memory discourse' (Huyssen, 2003), in that it seeks to convey the "essence" of Manchester through "two simple words that define what sets Manchester apart from our peers across the globe" (Marketing Manchester, 2009). Yet 'Original Modern' is also presented as incorporating a future-orientation in its perspective and potential— arguably another temporal characteristic of much place marketing/branding representation work. Thus, according to Marketing Manchester, 'Original Modern':

> …explains Manchester's spirit, its indefatigable energy for progress and change, that 'do something' attitude, that desire to be different that always has and always will exist within the city. Original Modern is what runs through Manchester's blood and it's detectable in the best of what we do.

And for Manchester to continue to manifest these values, Original Modern has to be an aspiration; an aspiration for all individuals, decision makers, groups, communities, organisations, and businesses that live, work and engage with Manchester.

(Marketing Manchester, 2009)

The (contested?) role of memory of the past in place marketing

Manchester's 'Original Modern' brand positioning gives an indication of how (selected) aspects of a place's past can be appropriated and accommodated within the representation work of place marketing and branding, and can thus be thought of as a 'memory discourse', whereby a particular "structuring of memory and temporality" (Huyssen, 2003, p. 15) is mobilized to help achieve a marketing-oriented vision for the place in question. Such activities could be seen as consistent with some critical trends in the discipline of human geography regarding the infusion of politics into place, where places become "both the product of, and a tool in, relations of power of one kind or another" (Cresswell and Hoskins, 2008, p. 394)—in this context, specifically relating to the influences on the content of particular place marketing messages.

Cresswell and Hoskins (2008) argue that place simultaneously evokes a certain materiality and also a less concrete realm of meaning. Regarding materiality, places inevitably have a tangible material form, either in terms of natural topographic features and/or a particular built environment. Indeed, as mentioned above (regarding, among other things, the designation of UNESCO World Heritage Site status), Cresswell and Hoskins note that the adjudication of what constitutes heritage landmarks and historic places "tends to focus entirely on the landscape functions of place—that is, functions that emphasize both materiality and the sense of sight" (ibid, p. 393). This resonates with the visual emphasis of much place marketing activity (see Hospers, 2009; Kotler et al., 1999) mentioned in the previous chapter. However, Cresswell and Hoskins (2008) also emphasize that places also evoke a less concrete realm of meaning, linked to lived experience in a place. Supporting this perspective, Alexander (1979) suggests that the life and soul of a place depend not merely on the physical environment but on the pattern of events experienced within it. Such sentiments are echoed in a personal reflection by American author Michael Pollan:

> ...when I think about spaces that I remember as having a strong sense of place, it isn't the "architecture" that I picture, the geometrical arrangements of wood and stone and glass, but such things as watching the world go by from the front porch of the general store in town, or the scuffle of ten thousand shoes making their way to work beneath Grand Central Station's soaring vault, or the guttering light of jack-o'-lanterns illuminating the faces of square dancers in a New England hayloft. The "design" of these places and the recurring events that give them their qualities—the spaces

and the times—have grown together in such a way that it is impossible to bring one to mind without the other.

(1997, p. 274)

Thus, materiality and the realm of meaning will come together in a particular location and will, moreover, be experienced through the different levels of practice and performance occurring therein, consistent with Cresswell and Hoskins' idea that place is "a lived concept" (2008, p. 394). Consequently, a place will be a source of memory for those who have experienced it. However, memory, as Cresswell and Hoskins note, "is conceived as a device that works to naturalize or (less often) contest existing social hierarchies" and in the latter case may occupy "a precarious ground at risk of becoming hidden, forgotten, silenced or shadowed by normative strategies of recall" (ibid: 394). Such 'normative strategies' can include the 'official' narratives that will be part of place marketing's representation work, which as has been seen earlier, can be very selective and potentially exclusionary, of those aspects of a place's history that are not consistent with the views of hegemonic groups, and which can—to all intents and purposes—be forgotten, even if the materiality of the place may give lie to such official neglect. Indeed, this (inter) relationship between the material and more intangible aspects of places will have significant implications for how places are represented in marketing and branding activities, potentially resulting in tensions between different ways in which the place is represented, especially in relation to the influence of temporality, which may be perceived differently among place stakeholders (see Reynolds et al., 2023).

Consequently, Reynolds et al. (2023) identify a number of 'temporal (re)framing strategies', which can be regarded as attempts to reconcile and/or challenge the connections between the past, the present (in terms of how the past is viewed), and the future vision of the place, as understood by different place stakeholders. Reynolds et al. identify two broad approaches to this task: *reconciliation* and *destabilization*.

With reconciliation, place stakeholders can try to reinterpret the privileging on a particular historical period through identifying broad themes that provide a thread of consistency between past, present and future, acting in essence as 'bridging narratives'. An alternative approach here, to the search for such similarity/consistency over time might be to try and differentiate by emphasizing 'bricolage', defined by Reynolds et al. in this particular place branding context as "the assembly of different elements across time-frames into a new representation as a strategy for garnering consensus" (2023, p. 8) through juxtaposing different place elements from different historical periods.

By contrast, some stakeholders might not seek reconciliation, but may seek to destabilize any consensus about place brand representation through the dissemination and enactment of their own 'confronting narratives', thereby highlighting existing tensions through their dissent (perhaps as a means of trying to change others' perspectives). An alternative approach identified by Reynolds et al. might be to 'differentiate' and separate the different place identities that have emerged over time—and in so doing potentially celebrating the place's diversity and dynamism.

These different approaches to incorporating the past into present representational strategies to achieve future-oriented visions (consistent with notions of omni-temporality mentioned in the more general branding literature) highlight how both temporal continuity and diversity may be incorporated into the representation work of place marketers and branders. Some potential implications arising from this dichotomy are discussed in the next chapter, introducing notions of *fluidity* and *fixity* in place marketing representation work.

References

Alexander, C. (1979). *The Timeless Way of Building*. Oxford and New York: Oxford University Press.

Bakare, L. (2023). The struggle for a black history of Manchester. *The Guardian*, 31 March. Available at: https://www.theguardian.com/news/ng-interactive/2023/mar/31/a-tale-of-two-cities-the-struggle-for-a-black-history-of-manchester [Accessed 10 October 2023].

BBC (2007). Slave trade shameful, Blair says. *BBC News Channel*, 25 March. Available at: http://news.bbc.co.uk/1/hi/uk/6493507.stm [Accessed 20 July 2018].

Bedell, G. (2011). The thirties restored. *The Observer Special Supplement – The King's Speech*, 9 January: Available at: https://www.theguardian.com/film/2011/jan/02/the-kings-speech-period-sets [Accessed 2 May 2024].

Benjamin, A., Block, R. Jr., Clemons, J., Laird, C. and Wamble, J. (2020) Set in stone? Predicting confederate monument removal. *Political Science and Politics*, 53(2): 237–242 http://dx.doi.org/10.1017/S1049096519002026

Broudehoux, A. M. (2001). Image making, city marketing and the aesthetization of social inequality in Rio de Janeiro. In N. Alsayyad (Ed.) *Consuming Tradition, Manufacturing Heritage*. Routledge: London, pp. 273–297.

Burch-Brown, J. (2022). Should slavery's statues be preserved? On transitional justice and contested heritage. *Journal of Applied Philosophy*, 39(5): 807–824. https://doi.org/10.1111/japp.12485

Carr, E. H. (1961). *What Is History?* Harmondsworth: Penguin Books.

Clegg, S. R. and Kornberger, M. (2010). An organizational perspective on space and place branding. In F. M. Go and R. Govers (Eds.) *International Place Branding Yearbook 2010: Place Branding in the New Age of Innovation*. Houndmills: Palgrave Macmillan, pp. 3–11.

Cresswell, T. and Hoskins, G. (2008). Place, persistence, and practice: Evaluating historical significance at Angel Island, San Francisco, and Maxwell Street, Chicago. *Annals of the Association of American Geographers*, 98(2): 392–413. https://doi.org/10.1080/00045600701879409

Dodge, M. (2020). Cotton. In P. Dobraszczyk and S. Butler (Eds.) *Manchester – Something Rich and Strange*. Manchester: Manchester University Press, pp. 113–117.

Drayton, R. (2019). Rhodes must not fall? Statues, postcolonial 'heritage' and temporality. *Third Text*, 33(4-5): 651–666. https://doi.org/10.1080/09528822.2019.1653073

Frigerio, A. (2021). The fate of statues of Stalin in post-soviet countries: Some critical reflections on the management of contested cultural heritage. *Heritage & Society*, 12(2–3): 136–150. https://doi.org/10.1080/2159032X.2021.1909416

Ghostsigns (2008). Jack Daniel's. Ghostsigns Blog, 18 January. Available at: Jack Daniel's | Ghostsigns [Accessed 16 January 2023].

Griffiths, R. (1998). Making sameness: Place marketing and the new urban entrepreneurialism. In N. Oatley (Ed.) *Cities, Economic Competition and Urban Policy*. London: Paul Chapman Publishing, pp. 41–57.

Historic England (2023). About us. Available at: https://historicengland.org.uk/about/ [Accessed 30 October 2023].

Hospers, G. J. (2009). Lynch, Urry and city marketing: Taking advantage of the city as a built and graphic image. *Place Branding and Public Diplomacy*, 5(3): 226–233. http://dx.doi.org/10.1057/pb.2009.10

Huyssen, A. (2003). *Present Past: Urban Palimpsests and the Politics of Memory*. Stanford: Stanford University Press.

Kotler, P., Asplund, C., Rein, I. and Haider, D. (1999). *Marketing Places Europe: Attracting Investments, Industries, Residents and Visitors to European Cities, Communities, Regions and Nations*. Harlow: Financial Times Prentice Hall.

Leask, A. (2006). World Heritage Site designation. In A. Leask and A. Fyall (Eds.) *Managing World Heritage Sites*. Oxford: Butterworth Heinemann, pp. 6–19.

Marcoux, J. S. (2016). Souvenirs to forget. *Journal of Consumer Research*, 43(6): 950–969. https://doi.org/10.1093/jcr/ucw069

Marketing Manchester (2009) *Original Modern*. Available at: http://www.marketing-manchester.com/wp-content/uploads/2017/02/OriginalModern.pdf [Accessed 5 March 2019].

Morgan, D. (2018). Soldier statues and empty pedestals: Public memory in the wake of the confederacy. *Material Religion*, 14(1): 153–157. https://doi.org/10.1080/17432200.2017.1418231

Pollan, M. (1997). *A Place of My Own: The Architecture of Daydreams*. London and New York: Penguin Books.

Reynolds, L., Peattie, K., Koenig-Lewis, N. and Doering, H. (2023). There's a time and place: Navigating omni-temporality in the place branding process. *Journal of Business Research*, 170: 114308. http://dx.doi.org/10.1016/j.jbusres.2023.114308

Ricoeur, P. (1984) *Time and Narrative Volume 1* (trans. K. McLaughlin and D. Pellauer). Chicago and London: The University of Chicago Press.

Roberts, S. and Read, R. (2021). *Ghost Signs: A London Story*. Fordingbridge: Isola Press.

Ross, D., Saxena, G., Correia, F. and Deutz, P. (2017). Archaeological tourism: A creative approach. *Annals of Tourism Research*, 67: 37–47. https://doi.org/10.1016/j.annals.2017.08.001

Sadler, D. (1993). Place marketing, competitive places and the construction of hegemony in Britain in the1980s. In G. Kearns and C. Philo (Eds.) *Selling Places: The City as Cultural Capital Past and Present*. Oxford: Pergamon Press, pp. 175–192.

Schutt, S. (2017). Rewriting the book of the city: On old signs, new technologies, and reinventing Adelaide. *Urban Geography*, 38(1): 47–65. https://doi.org/10.1080/02723638.2016.1139878

Schutt, S., Roberts, S. and White, L. (2017). *Advertising and Public Memory: Social, Cultural and Historical Perspectives on Ghost Signs*. New York and London: Routledge.

Short, J. R. (1999). Urban imagineers: Boosterism and the representation of cities. In A. E. G. Jonas and D. Wilson (Eds.) *The Urban Growth Machine: Critical Perspectives Two Decades Later*. New York, NY: State University of New York Press, pp. 37–54.

Stage, W. (1989). *Ghost Signs - Brick Wall Signs in America*. Cincinnati: ST Publications Inc.

Stephenson, B., Gournet, M. A. and Burch-Brown, J. (n/d). *Reviewing Contested Statues, Memorials and Place Names. Guidance for Public Bodies*. Available at: https://research-information.bris.ac.uk/ws/portalfiles/portal/309734885/Guidance_ for_public_bodies_reviewing_contested_heritage_2_.pdf [Accessed 20 September 2023].

UNESCO (2005). World Heritage List The criteria for selection. Available at: https://whc.unesco.org/en/criteria/ [Accessed 15 Feb 2019].

Warnaby, G. (2019). Of time and the city: Curating urban fragments for the purposes of place marketing? *Journal of Place Management and Development*, 12(2): 181–196. http://dx.doi.org/10.1108/JPMD-08-2018-0063

Warnaby, G. and Medway, D. (2017). Ghost fascias: Retail corporate identity revenants in urban space. In S. Schutt, L. White and S. Roberts (Eds.) *Advertising and Public Memory: Historical, Social and Cultural Perspectives on Ghost Signs*. London and New York: Routledge, pp. 173–186.

4 Fluidity and fixity

Introduction

The discussion in the previous chapter regarding place as constituting both materiality and a less tangible 'realm of meaning' (Cresswell and Hoskins, 2008) reveals a potential temporal paradox, which may have significant place marketing implications—not least in terms of how different place stakeholders regard the use of the past in place marketing and branding activities (see Reynolds et al., 2023). On the one hand, a relational understanding of place, as implied in the notion of places as inevitably 'provisional' (Cresswell, 2004), resonates with how, in a place marketing context, places as 'products' are assembled from a menu of contributory elements—akin to the notion of bricolage—to suit the particular requirements of different types of place users, consistent with marketing principles of segmentation, targeting and positioning (see Ries and Trout, 2001).

Yet at the same time, the materiality of place provides a stabilizing presence (Cresswell and Hoskins, 2008). Anderson (2012) describes this latter perspective as more 'sedentary' (as opposed to the potential dynamism implied in the relational understanding of place mentioned above). Consequently, he argues, places are 'static' in both location *and* temporality. Thus, places can be presented as "changeless, preserved and constant", meaning they "may grow or contract but remain more (or less) of the same" (ibid, p. 572). A critical issue here, discussed by Anderson, is that place *identity* is arguably created by temporal *continuity* which has a stabilizing effect, developed by a collective accretion of understanding built up over time—resonating with Cresswell and Hoskins' (2008) notion of places evoking a particular 'realm of meaning'. These processes thus render place identities that are characterized by durability, and as a consequence, potentially widely recognized and associated with the locale. As a result, they have the potential for appropriation into place marketing representation work seeking to differentiate the place in question from other, competing locations. Thus, even if the materiality of a place is constantly changing (for example, through redevelopment of the built environment), or if the place 'product' elements are constantly being reshuffled

DOI: 10.4324/9781032689937-4

like a pack of cards by place marketers to attract different types of place users, other more intangible aspects will remain, demonstrating a significant continuity. Referring to the urban context, Madanipour notes that:

> …even when a city changes beyond recognition, it still keeps some of its old characters in a kind of unconscious realm, through small traces that are left here and there, and in habits and routines, concepts and beliefs that people carry with them and share in their social life. Without being visible, this unconscious realm maintains a degree of continuity in society, even when the city's fabric and social institutions have significantly changed.
>
> (2017, p. 90)

Accordingly, in the specific context of place marketing representation work, I suggest that places have an essential temporal duality comprising:

(1) *fluidity*—in the sense that combination(s) of place attributes are inherently relational, open to being dynamically (re)assembled through time to create a particular place 'product' aimed to appeal to a specific audience (and here, the product being marketed could be regarded as pluriform in nature, reflecting the complex and kaleidoscopic nature of place);

and,

(2) *fixity*—which serves to differentiate from other places in an increasingly intense spatial competition. It is ineluctably temporal in nature; principally because it accretes—and endures—*over time* to provide a sense of permanence and stability, and from which a more robust sense of place identity can be created.

However, the binary nature of this fluidity and fixity can be overstated. As previously mentioned, from a temporal perspective, the enduring qualities of place are multiple and dynamic, and relational qualities are also profuse. There is a tension between producing an identifiable (and singular) place image for marketing and branding purposes (which, argue Clegg and Kornberger, 2010, is inevitably an oversimplification of a more complex and polyphonic reality), whilst also acknowledging and promoting the multiplicity of place through the assemblage of different place product elements (which in turn might constitute multiple 'realms of meaning', depending on the perspective from which a place is experienced). With specific reference to the role of temporality in place branding activity, these tensions are identified by Reynolds et al. (2023) in their discussion of different 'temporal (re)framing strategies', discussed at the end of the previous chapter. Moreover, the extent of this tension may wax and wane as a place inevitably changes and develops over time, with a promoted image and/or brand reflecting the reality of a place to a greater or lesser degree as time passes and the place itself changes—and also as the relative importance placed on history and heritage by place stakeholders (including marketing and branding professionals) may change over time.

These notions of fluidity and fixity—described by Cresswell and Hoskins (2008) in terms of the copresence of stability and change—can be illustrated and explicated in the context of place marketing through the example of a particular place product; namely Hadrian's Wall, in the north of England, as discussed below.

Hadrian's Wall

Hadrian's Wall is an archetypal 'fuzzy' place (Warnaby et al., 2010), which stands in contrast to what may be termed 'discrete' place entities such as nations, cities/towns—and at a smaller spatial scale, neighbourhoods and/ or other particular areas within them (such as Business Improvement Districts, or BIDs, for example—see Ward, 2007)—which are clearly delineated through jurisdictional boundaries, whether related to formal governance structures (such as local public administrations) or some other type of place management structure (such as BIDs). These boundaries, whilst sometimes disputed, define the spatial extent of the place 'product' being marketed in that they constitute the jurisdictional boundaries of the agencies responsible for the marketing activity and/or political administrative areas, which as mentioned above, may be manifested at a variety of spatial scales (Warnaby and Medway, 2021).

By contrast, the boundaries of 'fuzzy' places may be much more amorphous. Regions, for example, are spatial entities that may be shaped as much by symbols, social practice and consciousness (which according to Paasi, 2002, may emerge and develop over time, existing through a process of 'institutionalization'), as by discrete territorial boundaries (see Paasi, 2002, 2010—and also Hospers, 2004, 2006, with particular reference to the Oresund region). As I discuss below, delineating the spatial entity that constitutes 'Hadrian's Wall' for the purposes of its marketing and branding is fraught with complexity, but first I provide some contextual detail of the place and its management.

Management context

Dudley (1970) describes Hadrian's Wall as the most spectacular and best known Roman *limes* or frontier system (see Breeze and Dobson, 2000, for a detailed account of the building of, and life on, the Wall). It has been the subject of much antiquarian interest (see Hingley, 2012, for an extensive post-Roman history of the Wall) and has one of the longest traditions of conservation efforts relating to historical monuments in the UK (see Mason et al., 2003; Young, 2006, for more detail). In 1987, it was inscribed as a UNESCO

World Heritage Site (WHS), within the 'Frontiers of the Roman Empire' designation (which also includes the Antonine Wall in Scotland and the Upper German-Raetian Limes—see https://whc.unesco.org/en/list/430/). This designation, according to Mason et al., led to the Wall being viewed "more as a conceptual entity than as a particular place" (2003, p. 13) and also entailed the development of a Management Plan to facilitate coordination between the various local authorities, governmental agencies, organizations and groups that were stakeholders in the Wall.

Dating from AD122, the Wall stretches across the narrowest part of England, from the River Tyne in the east of the country to the Solway Firth in the west. Along its length are a series of milecastles and larger forts, the best known of which are Housesteads and Chesters. Nesbitt and Tolia-Kelly (2009) describe Hadrian's Wall as a 'linear monument', and it passes through numerous local authority jurisdictional areas, as well as a designated National Park, which creates its own problems as ownership of the Wall is fragmented. Indeed, there are various heritage organizations which are stakeholders in the Wall. English Heritage (a UK government-backed organization which preserves and protects monuments of national interest) owns and manages key sites along the Wall, and has overall responsibility for WHS Management Plan coordination. Natural England and the National Trust also own and/or manage some key sites along the Wall.

Before the 1970s, "there was little attempt to visualise the Wall as an entity, and to manage it as such" (Young, 2006, p. 207). In recent years this has changed, in part catalyzed by its WHS inscription and the consequent requirement for a management plan. The initiation of the Management Plan process (led by English Heritage) began in 1993, thereby creating "institutions and partnerships to manage the Wall and setting resources in ways that were coherent geographically and across sectors" (Mason et al.,2003, p. 18). Young (2006) states that the Management Plan has resulted in a more holistic approach to the management of Hadrian's Wall as a singular entity, and has also stimulated investment (primarily related to access and sustainable tourism).

The content of the second iteration of the WHS Management Plan (Austen and Young, 2002), covering the period 2002-2007, was influenced by the 2001 outbreak of Foot and Mouth disease which had a major impact on the area's rural economy. This in turn catalyzed the publication in 2004 of the *Hadrian's Wall Major Study Report*, commissioned by the two regional development agencies in the north of England at the time—the North West Development Agency (NWDA) and One North East (ONE). The aim of this report was "to assess the potential of Hadrian's Wall to support the regeneration of the North of England through the growth of tourism revenues and to deliver a new Vision for Hadrian's Wall" (North West Development Agency/One NorthEast [NWDA/ONE], 2004, p. 1).

There was an overt place marketing motivation underpinning the proposed activities outlined in the report, which articulated the following goal/vision:

"To move Hadrian's Wall from a Northern 'ought to see' to a Global 'must see, stay and return for more'" (NWDA/ONE, 2004, p. 4). This vision was to be achieved by positioning the Wall as the 'Greatest Roman Frontier'. Subsequently, in 2005, it was proposed that the organizational entity responsible for the Wall should be a non-charitable, not-for-profit company limited by guarantee, and in May 2006, Hadrian's Wall Heritage Limited (HWHL) was created, with the aim:

> To realise the economic, social and cultural regeneration potential of the Hadrian's Wall World Heritage Site and the communities and environment through which it passes by sustainable tourism development, management and conservation activities which benefit local communities and the wider region. And all that done in a way that reflects the values embodied in the World Heritage Site Management Plan.
>
> (HWHL, 2007, p. 1)

'Hadrian's Wall country'

In this particular spatial context, 'fixity' exists through the persistence of the material presence of the Wall (and its associated forts, and other Roman remains), especially in its rural central section. Hadrian's Wall also passes through urban areas (particularly the Tyneside conurbation) where its materiality is minimal as a result of later development, although its route has to some extent rematerialized via way-marking signs as part of a long-distance 'National Trail' footpath (Witcher et al., 2010). The emphasis on materiality is consistent with perceptions of historical significance (Cresswell and Hoskins, 2008), and also its designation as such by bodies such as UNESCO (Leask, 2006).

This materiality is also significant in the articulation—and development—of the Hadrian's Wall place 'product'. Drawing on mainstream marketing theory which conceptualizes a product offering as consisting of different levels, incorporating *core*, *supplementary* and *complementary* features (although specific terminology regarding these different levels of product may vary—see for example Baines et al., 2022; Kotler et al., 2023), Warnaby et al. (2010, 2011) conceptualize the nature of the Hadrian's Wall 'product' as constituting these three levels, as follows:

> *Core*—i.e. The Wall itself and associated forts and milecastles; in other words, the primary Roman attractions.
>
> *Supplementary*—i.e. Roman–related aspects constituting the broader Roman Frontier area delineated by the World Heritage Site, including museums and exhibitions with a strong Roman component.
>
> *Complementary*—i.e. The panoply of non-Roman attractions and contemporary tourism oriented businesses located within 'Hadrian's Wall Country', which is the term for the wider area used by those responsible

for its marketing (which is discussed in more detail below). At this level, the area becomes more of a heterogeneous tourist space (Edensor, 2007), where visits to the area can be motivated by reasons other than its Roman heritage.

There is an inevitable temporal dimension evident in the classification of product levels in this particular context. The material heritage constituting the core product is inevitably the oldest product element, with the supplementary product elements being more recent. Although it can be argued that all may not be as it seems—for example, in the 19th century, the landowner John Clayton systematically bought up farms along the line of the central section of Hadrian's Wall and set about 'restoring' the Wall on his estate by building a dry-stone wall from fallen stones over the surviving Roman material which was then capped with turf (Young, 2006). The resulting structure, known archaeologically as the 'Consolidated wall' or 'Clayton's Wall', has become synonymous with Hadrian's Wall (Witcher et al., 2010). Moreover, the continued material presence of the stone from which Hadrian's Wall is built is more complicated, and perhaps more dissipated than most visitors to the area realize, given that the Wall was an obvious source of raw material for field wall and farm buildings in the area in the post-Roman period (Young, 2006).

The complementary product elements, comprising the various non-Roman attractions and tourism oriented businesses are the perhaps the most recent, with the constellation of these elements in frequent flux, with the creation and cessation of businesses and activities. These complementary elements arguably constitute an assemblage of place product attributes and features, the specific permutation of which (including other Roman and Roman-related attributes in the other two product levels), will be enjoyed by individual visitors to the area depending upon their specific interests and leisure pursuits. This notion of assemblage is alluded to in promotional material developed by Hadrian's Wall Heritage Limited, which emphasizes the amount and variety of contributory place product elements (from the three product 'levels' above) in 'Hadrian's Wall Country'. This is described in one advertisement in terms of, "one epic adventure", which incorporates "25 Roman forts and museums,… 89 historic houses and museums, 38 art galleries, 469 places to stay, 273 cafes, 802 restaurants and 1004 pubs".

However, the actual delineation of spatial area containing all these elements—marketed as 'Hadrian's Wall Country'—appears somewhat indeterminate; in other words, it is an archetypal 'fuzzy' place. At one level, one can define Hadrian's Wall through the materiality of the Roman remains (and the 2002 WHS Management Plan contains an explicit cartographical representation of the spatial extent of the WHS designation). But the territorial extent of Hadrian's Wall *Country* (as a concept actively marketed by various Wall stakeholders) is less clear, and resonates with Brighenti's (2010) notion of a territory as being defined as much by patterns of relations and the practices that occur within a space, as by specific jurisdictional boundaries of those organizations/agencies that might administer the space. Thus, according to Brighenti, territories are both functional *and* expressive, and in the specific context of Hadrian's Wall the delineation of the 'place' being marketed is articulated in an 'expressive' manner (as Hadrian's Wall Country), consistent with Cresswell and Hoskins' (2008) notion of place as having a more phenomenologically oriented 'realm of meaning'.

Thus, Hadrian's Wall Country could be construed and seen as a manifestation of Paasi's (2010) notion of regions as social constructs, which emerge, develop and exist through a process of 'institutionalization' (Paasi, 2002). Such institutionalization is, Paasi argues, the outcome of the simultaneous and interconnected working of the following four different forces (or what he terms, 'shapes'):

> *The territorial shape*—i.e. the degree to which an area is distinct from other areas in spatial terms. A key question here is the extent to which territorial borders are clearly defined, recognisable (or even agreed upon), or whether the spatial remit of the region is 'fuzzy'.
>
> *The symbolic shape*—i.e. the development of regional symbols, such as its toponym (or place name), flag, and its cartographic depiction; in other words, the visible aspects of a region that may evoke a shared feeling.
>
> *The institutional shape*—i.e. the institutions that maintain the territorial and symbolic shape of a region. Examples include the formation of administrative bodies, educational centres and development agencies—and arguably, place management and marketing agencies.
>
> *The shape connected with the identity of an area*—i.e. the extent to which the region is "rooted" in the consciousness and social practices of people, and whether there is a particular regional identification by individuals and groups. In place marketing terms this could also include the constructed identity of the region *per se* (i.e. its desired reputation or brand), especially through the way(s) in which it is differentiated from other areas.

In the case of Hadrian's Wall country, some of these 'shapes' are arguably stronger than others. While the marketing activity seeks to convey the desired market positioning of the 'Greatest Roman Frontier' (NWDA/ONE, 2004) through HWHL's representation work, the region's territorial shape is somewhat 'fuzzy' and the institutional shape is arguably fragmented, consisting of a range of stakeholders, some of whom have contradictory outlooks and aims— what Warnaby et al. (2010) have termed jurisdictional, functional and strategic 'fissures' in the Wall. Arguably, the shape concerned with the identity of an area has an inevitable temporal dimension, implicit in Paasi's description of such identity being established "in social practices and consciousness, both internally and externally" (2002, p. 140), the accretion of which over time hopefully allowing regional identity to cohere. The development of the positioning concept of 'Hadrian's Wall Country' drawing on the enduring Roman heritage to promote the area is perhaps indicative of Cresswell and Hoskins' contention that such material endurance "provides an anchor for stories that circulate in and around a place" (2008, p. 395)—and such stories can be incorporated within (or indeed could actually constitute) place marketing narratives. Yet coexisting with this obduracy of place which serves to cement its particular character (and in marketing terms, hopefully differentiate it from other, competing places) are other contemporary attributes and elements which are more 'fluid', as a consequence of their ever-changing configurations—such as the bricolage of "469 places to stay, 273 cafes, 802 restaurants and 1004 pubs" promoted as being part of 'Hadrian's Wall Country—and which will contribute to a constantly changing assemblage of place product elements, contingent on the particular needs of different sets of place users.

Resonating with the work of Paasi (2002) at the level of the region, Kavaratzis and Kalandides (2015) describe four 'constitutive elements' of place more generally, which can give rise to the place-based associations that they regard as fundamental to place brands. These constitutive elements comprise:

Materiality—i.e. the material-physical substrate of social relations, consisting of place-bounded artefacts and of the human body; and according to Kavaratzis and Kalandides, this also "functions as crystallized history and materializes collective memory" (ibid, p. 1373).

Practices—i.e. the structures of social interaction in relation to the material substrate, including the production, use, and appropriation of materiality.

Institutions—i.e. the institutionalized and normative regulation system, which mediates between the material substrate of social space and social practices involved in its production, appropriation, and use; and can relate to power relations, legal regulation and social and aesthetic norms.

Representations—i.e. the spatial systems of signs, symbols and representation linked to the material substrate, including formal conceptions of place (such as toponyms, maps etc.), but which "also extend to all structures and elements than intentionally convey meaning related to the place" (Ibid, p. 1374)—which could obviously include the representation work of place marketing and branding.

Kavaratzis and Kalandides note that both power relations and time permeate all of these elements, resulting in constant tension and change. This is evident with regards to Hadrian's Wall with the complexity of the organizational structures for its management (resulting from the multiplicity of actors with a stake in the Wall), and also through the omni-temporality that is evident in the way that the materiality of this 'fuzzy' place has emerged over time, over the course of many different historic periods. Reprising Reynolds et al.'s (2023) approaches to brand positioning in order to navigate the inevitable omni-temporality within the context of Hadrian's Wall, one can see some evidence of a 'one-dimensional freeze-frame' approach given the inevitable emphasis on the Roman period as this is arguably the cornerstone of the area's identity (as 'Hadrian's Wall Country'). However, there is also a 'panning across time-frames' evident in the way that the area is represented, perhaps to broaden its appeal beyond those visitors who are primarily attracted by the Roman heritage, to promote the kinds of attributes and activities that attract people to any similar rural area. Thus, the different 'layers' of time (relating to different periods in the history of the area) can be appropriated for the purposes of place marketing, as discussed in the next section.

The 'layering' of time?

The coexistence of place elements from different historical periods (especially in terms of the materiality of the built environment) is a manifestation of the idea of time being 'layered'—a notion that I will return to in subsequent chapters of this book. The idea of history as being concerned with different time spans was explored by French historian Fernand Braudel (1980 [1958]), who in his explication of the concept of the *Longue Durée* posited three layers of time. The first layer, the history of events (*l'histoire événementielle*), is as Braudel suggests, concerned with a short time span—in other words, "a surface disturbance, the waves stirred up by the powerful movement of tides" (1980 [1972], p. 3). He argues that "[t]raditional history, with its concern for the short time span, for the individual and the event, has long accustomed us to the headlong, dramatic, breathless rush of its narrative" (1980 [1958], p. 27). The second layer refers to economic and social history that emphasizes cyclical movement, "which lays open large sections of the past, ten, twenty, fifty years at a stretch ready for examination" (ibid, p. 27). The third layer comprises "a history to be measured in centuries this time: the history of the long, even of the very long time span, of the *longue durée*" (ibid, p. 27).

Madanipour (2017, p. 93) illustrates Braudel's ideas in an urban context with reference to real estate. He states that *land use* "may change from one day to the next, depending on how people decide to use a particular place" (i.e. *l'histoire événementielle*), but *building form* "is more resilient to change, as buildings have a longer life, which may last for generations". Finally, analogous to the *longue durée*, the *street pattern* of the place "is the most resilient as it can remain unchanged for centuries" (ibid, p. 93). Indeed, in many cities, the current morphology of street plans can date from medieval times or even further back in history, even though the buildings on either side of the streets may have been built and rebuilt in the intervening period, and the use(s) to which they have been put will have changed beyond recognition countless times from their original construction.

This layering of time is evident in the particular context of Hadrian's Wall, where the past coexists with the present. Thus, the major Roman forts, which have existed for almost two millennia, are surrounded by a modern tourist infrastructure of visitor centres, cafes and car parks. In the Newcastle conurbation, sections of Hadrian's Wall are visible in modern housing estates, and indeed, in some cases are focal points of the public space within these estates. As mentioned above, many of the farms and farm buildings in the rural central section of the Wall's route have appropriated stone from the Wall in their construction. All of this evidences the ideas behind the concept of the *Longue Durée* and highlights how the history of the area, evident in its continuing materiality, constitutes a 'stabilising persistence' and contributes to the 'realm of meaning' of the place (Cresswell and Hoskins)—and thus, demonstrates notions of *fixity* that are capitalized upon on marketing activity to convey the distinct character of the place in order to regenerate the economy of the area. Indeed, the current efforts at marketing the Wall and branding the area as 'Hadrian's Wall Country' (described by Warnaby et al., 2010, 2011) could be regarded as part of the history of events (*l'histoire événementielle*), as—to use Braudel's term—a "surface disturbance" (1980 [1972], p. 3). These continuing marketing efforts (see https://hadrianswallcountry.co.uk), constantly (re)creating assemblages of place product attributes and attractions in novel ways to attract visitors, are an indication of the ongoing *fluidity* that is an integral element of the creation of a place 'product'.

The above discussion perhaps hints at the complicated nature of time in this particular context, and the next chapter explores different aspects of the concept of time which are of relevance in a place marketing and branding context.

References

Anderson, J. (2012). Relational places: The surfed wave as assemblage and convergence. *Environment and Planning D: Society and Space*, 30: 570–587. http://dx.doi.org/10.1068/d17910

Austen, P. and Young, C. (2002). *Hadrian's Wall World Heritage Site Management Plan 2002-2007*. Hexham: English Heritage/Hadrian's Wall World Heritage Site Management Plan Committee. Available at: https://nationaltrails.s3.eu-west-2.amazonaws.com/uploads/2_management_plan_2002_to_2007.pdf [Accessed 16 January 2023].

Baines, P., Fill, C. and Page, K. (2022). *Marketing* (6th Edition). Oxford: Oxford University Press.

Braudel, F. (1980[1958]). History and the social sciences: The *Longue Durée* (trans. S. Matthews). *On History*. London: Weidenfeld and Nicolson, pp. 25–54. Originally published in *Annales E.S.C.* no. 4 (October-December 1958), Débats et combats: 725–753. No. 4 (October–December 1958), Débats et combats: 725–753.

Braudel, F. (1980[1972]). The Mediterranean and the Mediterranean world in the age of Philip II: Extract from the preface (trans. S. Matthews). *On History*. London: Weidenfeld and Nicolson, pp. 3–5.

Breeze, D. J. and Dobson, B. (2000). *Hadrian's Wall* (4th Edition). London: Penguin Books.

Brighenti, A. M. (2010). On territorology: Towards a general science of territory. *Theory, Culture & Society*, 27(1): 52–72. http://dx.doi.org/10.1177/0263276409350357

Clegg, S. R. and Kornberger, M. (2010). An organizational perspective on space and place branding. In F. M. Go and R. Govers (Eds.) *International Place Branding Yearbook 2010: Place Branding in the New Age of Innovation*. Houndmills: Palgrave Macmillan, pp. 3–11.

Cresswell, T. (2004). *Place: A Short Introduction*. Malden MA/Oxford/Victoria: Blackwell Publishing.

Cresswell, T. and Hoskins, G. (2008). Place, persistence, and practice: Evaluating historical significance at Angel Island, San Francisco, and Maxwell Street, Chicago, *Annals of the Association of American Geographers*, 98(2): 392–413. https://doi.org/10.1080/00045600701879409

Dudley, D. (1970). *Roman Society*. Harmondsworth: Penguin Books.

Edensor, T. (2007). Mundane mobilities, performances and spaces of tourism, *Social and Cultural Geography*, 8(2): 199–215. https://doi.org/10.1080/14649360701360089

Hadrian's Wall Heritage Ltd. (2007). *Hadrian's Wall Heritage Limited Strategic Plan March 2007*. Available at: http://www.hadrians-wall.org/ResourceManager/Documents/HWHL_Strategic_Plan_March_2007.pdf [Accessed 13 November 2008].

Hingley, R. (2012). *Hadrian's Wall: A Life*. Oxford: Oxford University Press.

Hospers, G. J. (2004). Place marketing in Europe – The branding of the Oresund region. *Intereconomics*, 39: 271–279. http://dx.doi.org/10.1007/BF03031785

Hospers, G. J. (2006). Borders, bridges and branding: The transformation of the Øresund region into an imagined space. *European Planning Studies*, 14: 1015–1033. https://doi.org/10.1080/09654310600852340

Kavaratzis, M. and Kalandides, A. (2015). Rethinking the place brand: The interactive formation of place brands and the role of participatory place branding. *Environment and Planning A*, 47(6): 1368–1382. https://doi.org/10.1177/0308518X15594918

Kotler, P., Armstrong, G. and Balasubramanian, S. (2023). *Principles of Marketing* (19th Edition). Harlow: Pearson.

Leask, A. (2006). World heritage site designation. In A. Leask and A. Fyall (Eds.) *Managing World Heritage Sites*. Oxford: Butterworth Heinemann, pp. 6–19.

Madanipour, A. (2017). *Cities in Time: Temporary Urbanism and the Future of the City*. London: Bloomsbury Academic.

Mason, R., MacLean, M. G. H. and de la Torre, M. (2003). *Hadrian's Wall World Heritage Site English Heritage: A Case Study*. Los Angeles: The Getty Conservation Institute.

Nesbitt, C. and Tolia-Kelly, D. (2009). Hadrian's wall – Embodied archaeologies of the linear monument. *Journal of Social Archaeology*, 9(3): 368–390. https://doi.org/10.1177/1469605309338428

North West Development Agency/One NorthEast [NWDA/ONE] (2004). *Hadrian's Wall Major Study Report Summary September 2004*. Newcastle-upon-Tyne: NWDA.

Paasi, A. (2002). Bounded spaces in the mobile world: Deconstructing regional identity. *Tijdschrift voor Economische en Sociale Geografie*, 93: 137–48.

Paasi, A. (2010). Regions as social constructs, but who or what 'constructs' them? Agency in question. *Environment and Planning A*, 42(10): 2296–2301. http://dx.doi.org/10.1068/a42232

Reynolds, L., Peattie, K., Koenig-Lewis, N. and Doering, H. (2023). There's a time and place: Navigating omni-temporality in the place branding process. *Journal of Business Research*, 170: 114308. http://dx.doi.org/10.1016/j.jbusres.2023.114308

Ries, A. and Trout, J. (2001). *Positioning: The Battle for Your Mind.* New York: McGraw Hill Professional.

Ward, K. (2007). Business improvement districts: Policy origins, Mobile policies and urban liveability. *Geography Compass*, 1(3): 657–72. http://dx.doi.org/10.1111/j.1749-8198.2007.00022.x

Warnaby, G., Bennison, D. and Medway, D. (2010). Notions of materiality and linearity: The challenges of marketing the Hadrian's Wall place product. *Environment and Planning A*, 42(6): 1365–82. https://doi.org/10.1068/a42481

Warnaby, G., Bennison, D. and Medway, D. (2011). Branding a Roman frontier in the 21st century. In A. Pike (Ed.) *Brand and Branding Geographies.* Cheltenham and Northampton MA: Edward Elgar, pp. 248–263.

Warnaby, G. and Medway, D. (2021). Conceptions of place: From streets and neighbourhoods to Towns, cities, nations and beyond. In N. Papadopoulos and M. Cleveland (Eds.) *Marketing Countries, Places, and Place-Associated Brands: Identity and Image.* Cheltenham and Northampton MA: Edward Elgar, pp. 1–25.

Witcher, R., Tolia-Kelly, D. and Hingley, R. (2010). Archaeologies of landscape: Excavating the material geographies of Hadrian's Wall. *Journal of Material Culture*, 15(1): 105–128. http://dx.doi.org/10.1177/1359183510355228

Young, C. J. (2006). Hadrian's Wall: Conservation and archaeology through two centuries. In R. J. A. Wilson (Ed.) *Romanitas: Essays on Roman Archaeology in Honour of Sheppard Frere on the Occasion of His Ninetieth Birthday.* Oxford: Oxbow Books, pp. 203–210.

5 Instrumental and existential temporality

Introduction

It is perhaps appropriate at this juncture to discuss in more detail the nature of time itself. Clearly, any discussion regarding how time has been perceived throughout history is beyond the scope of this volume—and indeed, has been explored in detail elsewhere. Turetzky (1998), for example, outlines the history of the philosophy of time from the Ancient Greeks to the modern day, discussing in detail the role of time in various ontological theories throughout history. Narrowing the focus to consider the concept of time in an urban spatial context, Madanipour (2017), in his book *Cities in Time*, distinguishes between *instrumental* and *existential* temporality, and I use this basic distinction to structure the discussion of the nature of time in this chapter, with specific reference to place marketing and branding activities.

Instrumental temporality

Madanipour defines instrumental temporality in terms of:

> ...how time has become treated as an instrument and an asset, how it has been subject to the pressures of acceleration in the process of globalization and how transience and ephemerality are the outcome of these pressures.
>
> (2017, p. 5)

Verhagen (2023) states that time has increasingly become an abstract and universal medium, to be understood in quantitative rather than qualitative terms. He notes that this tendency has been termed 'clock time', arising from the adoption of the mechanical clock as a means of controlling workers' time, as opposed to the rhythms of agricultural work and religious devotion that characterized pre-industrial times, citing Martineau, who argues that the formation of a labour market and the consolidation of social relations in which human labour is a commodity "represents a meeting point between capitalist relations and clock-time" (2015, p. 123). Resonating with the adage that 'time

DOI: 10.4324/9781032689937-5

is money', time is thus regarded as a social institution to which a numerical value can be ascribed. Such an instrumental view of time is also evident in the particular context of place marketing, with some significant implications, primarily in terms of place marketing *messages*, place marketing *activities*, place marketing *positioning*, and place marketing *missions*, which I discuss in more detail below.

Messages

Aspects of this instrumental perspective on temporality have become important themes of marketing *messages*, especially for towns and cities. The accessibility of urban places—facilitating and enabling the efficient use (and saving) of instrumental time—is a recurrent theme of many place marketing campaigns. Gold (1994) argues that a focus on transport in place marketing's representation work is important not only in economic terms (i.e. enabling more effective performance of businesses located in the place in question), but also psychologically in that it helps to assuage any possible doubts among inward investors that moving to a location perceived as isolated is equated with becoming uncompetitive. Thus, focusing within marketing messages on claims for the centrality of the place through superior communications (e.g. good access to motorway networks, rail systems and especially in the US, short distances from regional and national airports) helps to convey a perception of convenience and speed, thereby saving time (and by implication, cost) through effective infrastructure. Superior inter-urban connectivity can also be communicated through maps, even though the marketing imperative to accentuate the positive as far as location is concerned means that the accuracy of the cartographic representations used to promote such spatial accessibility may be highly dubious (see Monmonier, 1996, for numerous examples of such questionable practice).

Many of the common tropes used in place marketing representation work seek to emphasize accessibility and connectivity, arguably to capitalize upon notions associated with the efficient use and/or saving of instrumental time. Early work by Pocock and Hudson (1978) shows how places are often represented in promotional materials as a 'centre', 'heart', 'hub' or 'capital' and Gold (1994) provides numerous examples of this, such as the German city of Hamburg conveying itself as in 'the middle of Europe', or Finland promoting itself as part of 'an integrated Europe' and as a 'unique gateway' to Russia and the Baltic states, and—perhaps more implausibly—the island of Madeira's claim to be central to the 'Atlantic economy' of Europe, North America and Africa.

Time is also an inherent aspect of place marketing messages that are *future*-oriented—a common occurrence where the purpose of place marketing activity is to capture and/or capitalize upon *potential* economic development opportunities. Equally, places with a material historic presence frequently seek to appropriate this for economic gain through tourism visitation, which if too successful, can create temporally related capacity issues of 'overtourism'. These issues invariably require management, which comprises the second aspect of instrumental temporality, relating to place marketing *activities*.

Activities

There may often be certain times when places (especially tourism destinations) might need to *manage*—or indeed, *reduce*—demand rather than constantly try to increase visitation; in other words, engage in *demarketing*. The basic premise behind demarketing involves decreasing consumption of a product (Baker, 1998; Mercer, 1999) for whatever reason. In their original exposition on the topic, Kotler and Levy (1971) identify different types of demarketing, including: (1) 'general demarketing' (i.e. reducing the level of total demand, which may be appropriate in times of temporary product shortages, chronic overcapacity and product elimination); (2) 'selective demarketing' (i.e. discouraging demand from certain types of customers, which Beeton, 2003, regards as an inherent part of the process of market segmentation and targeting); and (3) 'ostensible demarketing' (i.e. appearing to discourage demand as a device for actually increasing it).

Discussing demarketing in a specific place context, Medway and Warnaby (2008) and Medway et al. (2011) distinguish between *passive* and *active* forms. Passive place demarketing could involve emphasizing particular place product attributes to market a location to certain customer segments, perhaps arising from the need to prioritize scarce marketing or other place resources. Thus, tourism places that market themselves as party destinations for young, single people may consequently—and inadvertently—discourage visits by families and older people who may prefer a less raucous location for their holidays. However, the social problems arising from such 'nuisance tourism' can also lead to more active forms of demarketing, such as the 'dissuasion' campaign developed by the municipality of Amsterdam, targeting British men aged 18 to 34, encouraging them to 'stay away' if they were likely to engage in antisocial behaviour during their time in the city (see Boztas, 2023).

Active place demarketing may often be an explicit temporary strategy, occurring over a discrete time window—for example, to manage and/or attempt to avert or reduce the impact of a crisis situation or other time-limited event (Medway and Warnaby, 2008—and resonating with Kotler and Levy's contention that demarketing may indeed be a temporary strategy in many cases). Thus, messages emanating from the organizing body of the London 2012 Olympics before the event, relating to possible transport and other infrastructure challenges within the city, dissuaded many non-Olympic visitors, creating significant implications for more general tourism and economic activity in the city (see Warnaby and Medway, 2014).

Other active demarketing rationales may be motivated by the temporal nature of demand, where places might be demarketed at certain times of the year in an attempt to spread visitor numbers over an extended period to help reduce the negative impacts of seasonality (Medway et al., 2011). These impacts could include overtourism, which has been a significant theme in the tourism literature in recent years (see for example, Capocchi et al., 2019; Dodds and Butler, 2019; Mihalic, 2020).

The need to 'demarket' a place (for whatever reason) can lead to place marketing strategies with both spatial and temporal dimensions. Spatially oriented activities identified by Medway et al. (2011) include 'diversion demarketing' (i.e. the promotion and marketing of—or redirection of visitors to—alternative place offers, usually close to the destination being demarketed). An obvious temporally oriented activity will be some form of differential pricing strategy, such as discounts for off-peak visitation and/or removal of concessionary prices for certain customer types (e.g. students or pensioners) at very busy times based on when they visit the place (Medway et al., 2011).

Market positioning

From a general marketing perspective, positioning can be defined in terms of the place that a brand occupies in the mind of the consumer (see Ries and Trout, 2001). In a place marketing context, a location may attempt to create particular associations that serve to differentiate it from its competitors to ensure it is regarded as unique with regard to particular dimensions, thereby providing some advantage in an increasingly intense spatial competition. Temporality could be one such dimension used to differentiate places. For example, the city of Strasbourg in north western France seeks to commodify a particular period of the year by describing itself as the 'Capital of Christmas'. The city has one of the oldest Christmas markets in Europe—visited by nearly two million people each year—which is a major attraction. The website of the office of tourism for the city and region describes it in the following terms:

> For over a month, Strasbourg is imbued with **a festive, spiritual ambiance with few parallels anywhere else in Europe**.
>
> **The holiday spirit in Strasbourg is truly unique**. The city is decked out for the festive season, the houses are beautifully decorated… and, at dusk, **the magic starts to happen**. The city is **a wonder to behold**. Amidst the twinkling lights, the cathedral stands tall, in all its glory.
>
> (Office de Tourisme de Strasbourg et sa Région, 2019, online. Original emphasis)

Another temporal positioning strategy is to position a locale in terms of a particular historical period. In the city of Manchester, UK, the 'Medieval Quarter' lies adjacent to the main city centre shopping district and is the area where modern Manchester originated. Manchester Cathedral and Chetham's School and Library (dating from the twelfth and fifteenth centuries, respectively), are at the heart of this area, which also incorporates architecture from a range of periods, from Victoria Railway Station, built in the 1840s, the Corn Exchange dating from 1897-1903, and the contemporary Urbis building (opened in 2002 and since 2012, the home of the National Football Museum). Despite the locale's architectural melange of historic and contemporary, it has been positioned as the 'Medieval Quarter' at the behest of the City Council, with medieval-type typescript in branding materials, in an attempt to create an identity for the area, to distinguish it from other city centre locales.

Missions

As mentioned above, place marketing can be thought of as inevitably future orientated (Kaefer, 2021). Here, those responsible for the governance and management of places will seek to enhance (or at least secure) the place's competitive position and performance (using whatever performance metrics are deemed appropriate) in an environment that is uncertain, but which may be influenced by their strategic actions and plans (Kotler et al., 1999). In the context of urban regeneration, Raco et al. (2008) argue that the 'politics of space-time' is concerned with questions such as *when* particular types of development take place and relating to the different stakeholder groups involved, *whose* time frames should be prioritized (and marginalized), and how practices should be governed and regulated. The answers to these questions, they argue, will influence the nature of the places in which development takes place.

Similarly with place marketing and branding, questions relating to the future shape and character of a locale, and how this is to be achieved (i.e. a 'vision' for the place) over time—and then represented to users and potential users—are crucially important. Here, the importance of developing a vision for the place—articulating what the place's stakeholders want their place to *be* (Kotler et al., 1999)—is a fundamental starting point for strategy formulation (see for example, Balakrishnan, 2009), which can then be translated into more concrete objectives to help integrate activities and prevent inconsistencies in policy-making (van den Berg and Braun, 1999). This enables those responsible for managing/marketing the place to integrate objectives and resources with changing opportunities, whilst being flexible enough to absorb external shocks and respond to new developments in the external environment (Kotler et al., 1999). This is summed up by van den Berg and Braun, who state that "[a]ny urban place marketing policy should fit into a broadly supported comprehensive vision and strategy, with a clear strategy of implementation" (1999, p. 997).

The strategic imperative for a clear implementation strategy—which should include very specific timescales for the achievement of particular activities, monitored through effective evaluation mechanisms—clearly resonates with Ricoeur's (1984) notion of *expectation* (in terms of articulating 'things to come') in his discussion of the relationship between present and future.

These four aspects of messages, activities, positioning and missions are indicative of an instrumental temporality in this particular context, evident in the notion of 'clock time'—or what Walter Benjamin (1969 [1950]) called 'homogenous, empty time'—which according to Verhagen, constitutes "the measurable time of schedules and deadlines, time that has to be put to use" (2023, p. 136).

Existential temporality

Turning, by contrast, to Madanipour's (2017) notion of *existential* temporality, the emphasis is on a personal sense—or 'lived experience'—of time, which is in itself a subjective concept linked to individual memory and identity. This emphasis on personal lived experience resonates with Heidegger's (1962) concept of *dasein*—a German word for existence, meaning 'to be here'. *Dasein* could be viewed as closely intertwined with temporality, as time is "not a series of nows, but a unifying factor for being-in-the-world" (Madanipour, 2017, p. 77), and which as Turetzky (1998) suggests, unites past and present based on lived experience. This notion of the *individual* experience of place is echoed from the early days of the place marketing literature—in 1993, discussing the nature of the place 'product' (and implicitly acknowledging the notion of assemblage in this context), Ashworth states that each act of place consumption "is an individual experience and thus of an individual and not a standardised product" (1993, p. 645). This acknowledges the inseparability of the production and consumption of the place product, meaning that each individual's experience of place is a unique event. Thus, the place product assembled by place marketers, constituting a set of often quite generalized elements and attributes, will potentially be consumed in very different ways according to the particular characteristics, requirements and preferences of the individual place consumer—which of course, may vary over time, even for the same person.

This overtly individualistic and phenomenologically oriented perspective, Madanipour argues, creates a problem relating to how a multitude of individuals' different senses of existential time (including how it relates to places) can be shared and mutually understood. He states that key features of this existential temporality are subjectivity, memory and identity, and that if these features are disrupted or lost, then it could result in "cultural amnesia, a sense of transience, loss of collective memory and fluidity and multiplicity in the common frameworks of meaning and identity" (2017, p. 75). These problems can, Madanipour argues, potentially be overcome through Husserl's notion of 'lifeworld', which has been defined by Pivcevic (1970) in terms of the realm of everyday life in which we live and share ideas and experiences with others. Put otherwise—and in the particular context of place marketing—seeking to understand the nature of shared and place-related temporal experiences, consistent with the 'lifeworld' concept (which emphasizes *common* experiences), could be fundamental in informing the representation work of place marketers in seeking to identify the 'essence' of a place. This can then be articulated and communicated in ways that resonate with actual and potential place users, perhaps through the creation of widely shared *associations* with the place in their minds—which is an important aspect of place brand creation (Kavaratzis and Kalandides, 2015; Zenker and Braun, 2017).

From a place marketing perspective, there is an inevitable temporal dimension to this discussion, linked to the notion of *fixity* introduced in Chapter Four. To reprise, fixity refers to aspects of place that accrete and endure over time to provide a sense of permanence and stability. As mentioned previously, such place aspects can be material (e.g. the built environment), but also more intangible—what Madanipour (2017) terms the 'unconscious realm' that relate to our memory and lived experience of place. This can be at both individual and collective levels. In the context of place branding, Aitken and Campelo highlight the importance of a *collective* construction of local identity and belonging arising from a synthesis of what they term the '4Rs', namely: *rights, roles, responsibilities* and *relationships*, which emerge "from the social capital or communal practices of the place that are re- and co-created through community engagement" (2011, p. 925), which can in turn reinforce engagement and relationships among the community. From such a collective understanding a more robust sense of place identity can arguably be created, thereby differentiating from other places, which in turn should facilitate the development of feelings of attachment to place, as felt by those who live and visit.

Place attachment—defined as "an affective bond or link between people and specific places" (Hidalgo and Hernández, 2001, p. 274) and reminiscent of Tuan's (1974) concept of *topophilia*—has been an important theme in the place marketing literature (see for example, Florek, 2011; Zenker and Rütter, 2014), and which has been equated to the general marketing concept of consumer brand loyalty (see Florek, 2011). Place attachment is influenced by various demographic, social, physical and symbolic factors (see for example, Florek, 2011; Hay, 1998; Hernández et al., 2007; Steadman, 2003)—and among these factors temporal aspects are important. These temporal aspects include length of residence (Fleury-Bahi et al., 2008; Florek, 2011; Hernández et al., 2007) and property ownership (Lalli, 1992), and are particularly strong if the place experience is positive (Hernández et al., 2007; Insch and Florek, 2008). Moreover, reflecting the deeper, phenomenologically oriented perspective that is inherent in the notion of existential temporality, focusing on the significance of place to human life, Relph (1976) notes that place attachment will vary in terms of shallowness and depth, dependent on such factors as the sense of community engendered, the sense of time involved and the value of 'rootedness'—all of which resonate with the notion of *fixity*. Emphasizing the inherent temporality of this, Relph states that a growing sense of place attachment will be imbued with a sense of continuity and "the feeling that this place has endured and will persist as a distinctive entity even though the world around may change" (1976, p. 31).

If place attachment arguably increases with length of residence (Fleury-Bahi et al., 2008; Florek, 2011; Hernández et al., 2007), then from a place marketing and branding perspective, residents could be both an important audience *for*—and also a potent positive element *of*—place marketing and branding initiatives. Warnaby and Medway (2013) acknowledge the dual role of residents in this regard—as both targets and (co)creators of place brands. Further, Braun et al. (2010) identify various roles that residents may play: as an integrated *part* of the place brand, through their characteristics and behaviour; as *ambassadors*, granting credibility to communicated messages; and finally, as *citizens and voters*, who are instrumental in the political legitimization of place branding.

Indeed, the importance of marketing to residents is increasingly acknowledged in the place marketing literature, and their role(s) in place marketing activities—often motivated by a strong sense of attachment to 'their' place—can be shown through events in the city of Manchester in 2011 (see Warnaby and Medway, 2013, for further details).

'I Love MCR'

On 9 August 2011, Manchester along with other cities in the UK endured rioting, which began in London a few days before in the aftermath of the police shooting of a man in the Tottenham area. The riots dominated regional and national media news coverage, and the potentially negative implications for how the affected places were now perceived were obvious to all. It was apparent that relevant place based authorities and agencies had a significant marketing task to do, if major reputational damage was to be averted.

In Manchester city centre, on the day after the riots an 'army' of approximately 1000 citizen volunteers (motivated by strong feelings of place attachment) turned out to help in a street clean-up, and in so doing became a symbol and channel of the fight-back against rioters and looters, which was reported extensively in local and regional media. This spontaneous response of concerned citizens was capitalized upon for a place marketing campaign with the theme 'I Love MCR' which was launched (primarily through social media) by Marketing Manchester and Manchester Arndale Shopping Centre, three days after the riots began. The logo 'I Love MCR' (with the word 'love' denoted by a red heart shape) appeared all over the city, from small stickers in shop windows, to large hoardings covering major buildings in the city, such as the CIS Tower and the Manchester Central Conference Centre. The logo itself imitated graphic designer Milton Glaser's seminal 'I Love NY' campaign for the city of New York in 1977, which was (at least in part) credited with pulling the city back from the brink of bankruptcy (Ward, 1998). Stubbs (2012) argues that this logo encapsulates a very simple and focused message relating to the passion that New Yorkers have for their city. Its ongoing efficacy in simply articulating a very strong focus of attachment to—and affection, or even love, for—a place is demonstrated in the way it is still used on all kinds of promotional material for the city, and in its serial replication (with modification for the name of the place in question) by countless other cities and towns across the world—including Manchester. Indeed, the press release announcing the 'I Love MCR' campaign is explicit in its evocation and articulation of the love for the city amongst its residents:

> Glen Barkworth, general manager at Manchester Arndale said: "The manner in which staff, retailers and the people on the streets of Manchester have responded to the atrocities of this week is exemplary of the true Mancunian spirit. This campaign embodies that and galvanises people in a common good cause which will put Manchester back on the map for all the right reasons.
>
> Andrew Stokes, chief executive of Marketing Manchester, said: "Mancunians are incredibly proud of their city. We have seen this in the extraordinary outpouring of emotion from the people of Greater Manchester. We saw it in response to the mindless violence on Tuesday and we have seen it in the way they took to the streets to clear-up the mess that was made".
>
> (Marketing Manchester, 2011, online)

During the first weekend after the riots there was a 'We Love MCR day', with various city centre activities. Over subsequent weeks, other initiatives (including a series of special events including free dance, street theatre and comedy) took place to attract shoppers and visitors back to the city centre. In addition, car parking charges in the city centre were waived at certain times, as were fares on the entire Metrolink urban transport system on particular days, in order to encourage people into the city centre. The Chief Executive of Manchester City Council exhorted city centre businesses to introduce their own incentives to attract customers: "If you can put on a special offer in your stores, bars and restaurants, it helps to get the message out that we are open for business, and will hopefully get people in and get people spending" (The Guardian, 2011, online).

This place marketing campaign was aimed squarely at residents, its aim being "to show the world that the people of Manchester are proud of their city and united against anti-social behaviour" (Marketing Manchester, 2011, online). In doing so, it obviously sought to capitalize upon strong feelings of topophilia and attachment to their home city amongst the city's population, whilst trying to repair damage to the local economy by encouraging shoppers back to the city centre in the immediate aftermath of the riots.

Time and place marketing

In summary, the 'I Love MCR' campaign illustrates, both explicitly and implicitly, the influence of time in place marketing activities. The motivation behind the campaign itself was related to the need to respond to a particular crisis situation faced by the city, and arguably time was of the essence in developing a response that sought to avoid significant reputational damage to the city as well as restoring the economic fortunes of many city centre's retail and hospitality industry businesses by restoring public confidence that the city centre was a safe place to visit. Thus, from an 'instrumental time' perspective, there was 'value' in acting quickly. From a more phenomenologically oriented 'existential time' perspective, the campaign capitalized upon deep-rooted feelings of place attachment and topophilia among the city's residents, which will be a function of time (Fleury-Bahi et al., 2008; Florek, 2011; Hernández et al., 2007) and feelings of rootedness (Relph, 1976).

This Manchester case study also highlights other ways in which notions of 'time management' might impact on place marketing and branding activities. Eshuis and van Buuren (2014) identify five aspects of time—namely, its *nature*, *rhythm*, *tempo*, *quantity* and *time horizon*—that may influence such activities.

Regarding the *nature* of time, Eshuis and van Buuren argue that if time is considered as sequential, then strategies may be aimed at phasing and organizing activities going forwards, distinguishing between monochronic (where activities take place sequentially), and synchronic processes (where different activities may run simultaneously). By contrast, if time is regarded as cyclical in nature, then activities may recur in cycles, perhaps relating to processes of planning, implementation and evaluation of activities. Eshuis and van Buuren also suggest that a more adaptive form of time management might more effectively accommodate the tempo and rhythm of the environment; so for example, planning cycles coinciding with critical junctures in time. Thus for example, the marketing and other activities of a Business Improvement District will be linked to the timespan that the organization has a mandate to operate, through the ballot process which is normally five years (see Grail et al., 2020, for more detail).

Eshuis and van Buuren (2014) suggest that tempo of activities can be influenced by an organization, being strategically increased (to accelerate action) or delayed (to slow down the pace of activity, perhaps in order to generate support as it progresses), as well as being used to synchronize with the activities of other organizations. Timing—relating to the actual point at which an activity occurs—is also important, as this may impact on possible success/failure. Indeed, the finite timescale of many place management organizations (such as BIDs) or the electoral cycles of place governance processes will influence the amount of time an organization or public administration has to 'get things done'. Linked to this is the management of horizons, relating to whether activities need to be planned in the short-, medium- or long-term, depending on circumstances.

With regards to these temporal aspects, identified by Eshuis and van Buuren (2014), the 'I Love MCR' campaign highlights the importance of a quick tempo of activities when time is limited, motivated by a situation which could have a significant negative effect on the place, both in reputational and economic terms. The limited time arguably necessitated the use of social media to rapidly disseminate marketing messages about a range of activities that took place synchronically (to maximize impact), given the short nature of the time horizons involved.

Thus, it can be argued that place marketing and branding initiatives, and the concomitant representation work, are inevitably influenced to a greater of lesser degree by temporal considerations. In the following chapter, I evaluate the implications for place marketing and branding theory and practice.

References

Aitken, R. and Campelo, A. (2011). The 4Rs of place branding. *Journal of Marketing Management*, 27(9–10): 913–933. http://dx.doi.org/10.1080/0267257X.2011.560718

Ashworth, G. J. (1993). Marketing of places: What are we doing? In G. Ave and F. Corsico (Eds.) *Urban Marketing in Europe*. Turin: Torino Incontra, pp. 643–649.

Baker, M. J. (1998). *Macmillan Dictionary of Marketing and Advertising*. Basingstoke and London: Macmillan Business.

Balakrishnan, M. S. (2009). Strategic branding of destinations: A framework. *European Journal of Marketing*, 43(5/6): 611–629. http://dx.doi.org/10.1108/03090560910946954

Beeton, S. (2003). Swimming against the tide – Integrating marketing with environmental management via demarketing. *Journal of Hospitality and Tourism Management*, 10(2): 95–107.

Benjamin, W. (1969[1950]). Theses on the philosophy of history. In *Illuminations* (trans. H. Zohn). New York: Schocken Books, pp. 253–264.

Boztas, S. (2023). Amsterdam tells young British men who want a 'messay' weekend to stay away. *The Guardian*, 28 March. Available at: www.theguardian.com/world/2023/mar/28/amsterdam-young-british-men-misbehave-stay-away-campaign [Accessed 12 January 2024].

Braun, E., Kavaratzis, M. and Zenker, S. (2010). My City - My Brand: The Role of Residents in Place Branding. Paper presented at the 50th European Regional Science Association Congress, Joenkoeping, Sweden.

Capocchi, A., Vallone, C., Pierotti, M. and Amaduzzi, A. (2019). Overtourism: A literature review to assess implications and future perspectives. *Sustainability*, 11(12): 3303. http://dx.doi.org/10.3390/su11123303

Dodds, R. and Butler, R. W. (2019). *Overtourism: Issues, Realities and Solutions*. Berlin and Boston: De Gruyter.

Eshuis, J. and van Buuren, A. (2014). Innovations in water governance: The importance of time. *International Review of Administrative Sciences*, 80(2): 401–420 https://doi.org/10.1177/0020852313514518

Fleury-Bahi, G., Félonneau, M. L. and Marchand, D. (2008). Processes of place identification and residential satisfaction. *Environment and Behavior*, 40(5): 669–682. https://doi.org/10.1177/0013916507307461

Florek, M. (2011). No place like home: Perspectives on place attachment and impacts on city management. *Journal of Town & City Management*, 1(4): 346–354.

Gold, J. R. (1994). Locating the message: Place promotion as image communication. In J. R. Gold and S. V. Ward (Eds.) *Place Promotion: The Use of Publicity and Marketing to Sell Towns and Regions*. Chichester: John Wiley & Sons, pp. 19–37.

Grail, J., Mitton, C., Ntounis, N., Parker, C., Quin, S., Steadman, C., Warnaby, G., Cotterill, E. and Smith, D. (2020). Business improvement districts in the UK: A review and synthesis. *Journal of Place Management and Development*, 13(1): 73–88. https://doi.org/10.1108/JPMD-11-2019-0097

Hay, R. (1998). Sense of place in developmental context. *Journal of Environmental Psychology*, 18(1): 2–29. https://psycnet.apa.org/doi/10.1006/jevp.1997.0060

Heidegger, M. (1962). *Time and Being*. Oxford: Blackwell.

Hernández, B., Hidalgo, M. C., Salazar-Laplace, M. E. and Hess, S. (2007). Place attachment and place identity in natives and non-natives. *Journal of Environmental Psychology*, 27: 310–319. https://doi.org/10.1016/j.jenvp.2007.06.003

Hildago, M. C. and Hernandez, B. (2001). Place attachment: Conceptual and empirical questions. *Journal of Environmental Psychology*, 21: 273–281. https://doi.org/10.1006/jevp.2001.0221

Insch, A. and Florek, M. (2008). A great place to live, work and play: Conceptualising place satisfaction in the case of a city's residents. *Journal of Place Management and Development*, 1(2): 138–149. https://doi.org/10.1108/17538330810889970

Kaefer, F. (2021). Place branding: The future. In F. Kaefer (Ed.) *An Insider's Guide to Place Branding: Shaping the Identity and Reputation of Cities, Regions and Countries*. Cham: Springer, pp. 43–47.

Kavaratzis, M. and Kalandides, A. (2015). Rethinking the place brand: The interactive formation of place brands and the role of participatory place branding. *Environment and Planning A*, 47(6): 1368–1382. https://doi.org/10.1177/0308518X15594918

Kotler, P. and Levy, S. J. (1971). Demarketing, yes, demarketing. *Harvard Business Review*, 79: 74–80.

Kotler, P., Asplund, C., Rein, I. and Haider, D. (1999). *Marketing Places Europe: Attracting Investments, Industries, Residents and Visitors to European Cities, Communities, Regions and Nations*. Harlow: Financial Times Prentice Hall.

Lalli, M. (1992). Urban-related identity: Theory, measurement, and empirical findings. *Journal of Environmental Psychology*, 12(4): 285–303. https://doi.org/10.1016/S0272-4944(05)80078-7

Madanipour, A. (2017). *Cities in Time: Temporary Urbanism and the Future of the City*. London: Bloomsbury Academic.

Marketing Manchester (2011). People of Manchester demonstrate their love for the city-region - Press release. Available at: http://www.marketingmanchester.com/media-centre/press-releases/12th-august-2011.aspx [Accessed 25 June 2012].

Martineau, J. (2015). *Time, Capitalism and Alienation: A Socio-Historical Inquiry into the Making of Modern Time.* Chicago: Haymarket Books.

Medway, D. and Warnaby, G. (2008). Alternative perspectives on marketing and the place brand. *European Journal of Marketing*, 42(5/6): 641–653. https://doi.org/10.1108/03090560810862552

Medway, D., Warnaby, G. and Dharni, S. (2011). Demarketing places: Rationales and strategies. *Journal of Marketing Management*, 42(1–2): 124–142. http://dx.doi.org/10.1080/02672571003719096

Mercer, D. (1999). *Marketing: The Encyclopaedic Dictionary.* Oxford: Blackwell Business.

Mihalic, T. (2020). Conceptualising overtourism: A sustainability approach. *Annals of Tourism Research*, 84: 103025. https://doi.org/10.1016/j.annals.2020.103025

Monmonier, M. (1996) *How to Lie with Maps* (2nd edition). Chicago and London: The University of Chicago Press.

Pivcevic, E. (1970). *Husserl and Phenomenology.* London: Hutchinson.

Pocock, D. and Hudson, R. (1978). *Images of the Urban Environment.* London and Basingstoke: The MacMillan Press.

Raco, M., Henderson, S. and Bowlby, S. (2008). Changing, times, changing places: Urban development and the politics of space—time. *Environment and Planning A*, 40(11): 2652–2673. https://doi.org/10.1068/a4073

Relph, E. (1976). *Place and Placelessness.* London: Pion.

Ricoeur, P. (1984). *Time and Narrative Volume 1* (trans. K. McLaughlin and D. Pellauer). Chicago and London: The University of Chicago Press.

Ries, A. and Trout, J. (2001). *Positioning: The Battle for Your Mind.* New York: McGraw Hill Professional.

Steadman, R. C. (2003). Is it really just a social construction? The contribution of physical environment to sense of place. *Society and Natural Resources*, 16: 671–685. https://doi.org/10.1080/08941920309189

Stubbs, J. (2012). *Wish You Were Here. The Marketing of Stockholm and Destinations.* Stockholm: UP There, Everywhere.

The Guardian (2011). The Northerner Blog: I Love Manchester campaign grows in strength. Available at: http://www.guardian.co.uk/uk/the-northerner/2011/aug/19/manchester-riots-fightback-shopping-campaign [Accessed 11 January 2012].

Tuan, Y. F. (1974). *Topophilia: A Study of Environmental Perception, Attitudes, and Values.* New York: Columbia University Press.

Turetzky, P. (1998). *Time.* London and New York: Routledge.

van den Berg, L. and Braun, E. (1999). Urban competitiveness, marketing and the need for organizing capacity. *Urban Studies*, 36(5–6): 987–999. https://doi.org/10.1080/0042098993312

Verhagen, M. (2023). *Viewing Velocities: Time in Contemporary Art.* London and New York: Verso.

Ward, S. V. (1998). *Selling Places: The Marketing and Promotion of Towns and Cities 1850-2000.* London: E & FN Spon.

Warnaby, G. and Medway, D. (2013). What about the 'place' in place marketing? *Marketing Theory,* 13(3): 345–363. https://doi.org/10.1177/1470593113492992

Warnaby, G. and Medway, D. (2014). Synchromarketing: Demarketing places. In N. Bradley and J. Blythe (Eds.) *Demarketing*. London and New York: Routledge, pp. 26–41.

Zenker, S. and Braun, E. (2017). Questioning a "one size fits all" city brand: Developing a branded house strategy for place brand management. *Journal of Place Management and Development*, 10(3): 270–287. https://doi.org/10.1108/JPMD-04-2016-0018

Zenker, S. and Rütter, N. (2014). Is satisfaction the key? The role of citizen satisfaction, place attachment and place brand attitude on positive citizenship behavior. *Cities*, 38: 11–17. https://doi.org/10.1016/j.cities.2013.12.009

6 Re-evaluating temporality in place marketing

Introduction

Given that time and place are intimately bound together in complex ways (Huyssen, 2003; Madanipour, 2017), there is arguably a pressing need to understand the role of time and temporality in relation to place marketing and branding. In this book, I have sought to demonstrate that place marketing and branding have an inevitable temporal dimension, both in terms of how places can be represented and in relation to the processes by which this activity is planned and implemented. The importance of temporality is especially evident when heritage is incorporated into the marketing and branding activities of those locations that have a unique historical built and natural environment. For example, a report by Historic England—an organization whose avowed aim is to help people care for, enjoy and celebrate England's historic environment—titled *Heritage and Place Branding*—states that heritage:

> …highlights the unique character of a place and plays an important part in shaping perceptions and authentic experiences of a place. Heritage has the potential to form a key element of place brands by providing authenticity, distinctiveness and credibility.
>
> (2016, p. 3)

Heritage can be both material, incorporating the built and natural environment, as in 'Hadrian's Wall Country' (discussed in Chapter 4), and also more intangible. This intangible heritage is evident in the habits and routines and the concepts and beliefs that people carry with them (Madanipour, 2017), which will be encapsulated in historical knowledge and stories about a place (Ross et al., 2017). Indeed, the Historic England report cited above emphasizes the importance of intangible heritage—in part because "the identity, uniqueness and character of places is not limited by the number or significance of [physical] heritage assets present" (Historic England, 2016, p. 14).

The importance of temporality is readily—albeit often implicitly—acknowledged, evidenced in the contribution of heritage to the broader

DOI: 10.4324/9781032689937-6

economic development of places and associated marketing/branding activities. However in this book, I argue for a broader and more nuanced appreciation of the role of time and temporality reflecting the fact that in any one place, temporality can be multi-layered with different historic periods immediately evident. This may be manifested in architecture from different periods of history co-existing in a cityscape as a consequence of piecemeal (re)development over time, as exemplified in Madanipour's description of the city of Newcastle upon Tyne, in the north-east of England, which is the eastern extent of Hadrian's Wall:

> If we stand on the riverside…we can look around and see the remnants of two thousand years of history. What is now called the Swing Bridge has replaced a Roman bridge over the river Tyne, a node on the wall that the emperor Hadrian built to protect his northernmost territories from the ancestors of the Scots. The straight and long streets such as Westgate are built along the wall, which ended in Wallsend further east. From this vantage point, we can see the Castle Keep, which was built a millennium ago after William conquered Britain and built many castles to dominate the country. We can see the remains of the medieval walls and streets of the city, and buildings from medieval Georgian and Victorian periods, as well as the twentieth and twenty-first centuries. From our vantage point, they are all episodes of the past, all traces of ideas and practices that we may no longer recognize.
>
> (2017, pp. 91–2)

Yet as mentioned above, there is also the less tangible heritage—or what Madanipour terms "the unconscious realm" (2017, p. 90)—which can suffuse through the place, contributing to its character and essence. The existence of this intangible heritage can, according to Ross et al. (2017), facilitate a more co-creative interpretation of the stories and knowledge associated with a place—which can in turn be appropriated for the purposes of place marketing and branding. This final chapter evaluates the role of time and temporality and points to future avenues for research in this somewhat neglected aspect of the place marketing and branding literature.

Evaluating temporality?

As discussed in Chapter 4, there exists this copresence of stability and change (Cresswell and Hoskins, 2008) with the past and present coexisting in a particular place, demonstrating temporal fixity and fluidity. In part, this is a consequence of what has been termed the *multilayering* of time in this spatial context. Such notions of temporal multiplicity—and the consequent juxtaposition of the past and present in the same place—are consistent with Michel Serres' notion of time 'percolating', rather than flowing in a linear manner.

Here, Serres uses the analogy of the flow of the River Seine to describe this phenomenon:

> Yes, time flows like the Seine, if one observes it well. All the water that passes under the Mirabeau Bridge will not necessarily flow into the English Channel; many little trickles turn back towards Charenton or upstream.
> (Serres with Latour, 1995, p. 58)

Serres states that the flow of water is not laminar (i.e. fluid molecules following smooth paths in layers, with little or no mixing), and that, like water, time also flows in a similarly "turbulent and chaotic manner; it percolates" (ibid, p. 59).

This percolation analogy helps capture the inherent complexity of the different paces with which change happens in a place, with implications for the social and power relations that exist there (see Crinson and Tyrer, 2005). Temporal percolation, Serres argues, "can be schematized by a kind of crumpling, a multiple, foldable diversity" (Serres with Latour, 1995, p. 59), and its implications for the narratives of place marketing representation work can be advanced using Doel's (1996, 1999) concept of *scrumpled geographies*. Highlighting the potential turbulence of the percolation process, Doel presents still-visible remnants of the past as *disjointures* and uses terms such as 'folds', 'intervals' and 'joints' to highlight different facets of interlaced (dis)continuities in space and time. Considering this—and Serres' notion of percolating time—in the context of Madanipour's description of Newcastle upon Tyne cited above, then past 'events' still visible through their material presence in the built environment (i.e. the Swing Bridge, the Castle Keep etc.) can be considered as space-time disjointures (as might be the ghost signs discussed in Chapter 3). These disjointures arguably contribute to the ongoing creation of place as an "open end process" (Kalandides, 2011, p. 36), and echo Cresswell's contention that places "are never 'finished' but are constantly being performed" (2004, p. 37).

These processes are evident in the Belval neighbourhood located in the west of Esch-sur-Alzette, in south-western Luxembourg, in the heart of the country's mining district. Belval is dominated by the old steelworks, dating from the beginning of the twentieth century (see Figure 6.1). The steelworks ceased production in 1997, turning West Belval into an industrial wasteland. However in the intervening period, the 120 hectare site has been the subject of a 450 million Euros regeneration programme to establish the 'City of Science', incorporating a large cultural and scientific centre, including the science faculty of the University of Luxembourg. After an international urban planning contest to outline the future of the area in 2001, a masterplan produced by architects and urbanists Jo Coenen & Co proposed five neighbourhoods; residential districts in North and South Belval, a public park (Park Belval), Square Mile (including shops, offices and housing) and the Blast

Figure 6.1 Part of the old blast furnaces at Belval, Luxembourg. Photograph by the author.

Furnaces Terrace (including the City of Science, which revolves around two poles: the university centre around the Maison du Savoir (House of Knowledge) in the north; and the social and cultural centre around the blast furnaces in the south).

Considering this through the lens of Lefebvre's (1991) spatial triad of the *perceived*, the *conceived* and the *lived*, masterplans such as this could be regarded as *conceived* space, described by Lefebvre as "conceptualized space, the space of scientists, planners, urbanists, technocratic subdividers and social engineers" (ibid, p. 38). In her discussion of the 'timescapes of urban change' (which adopts an explicitly temporal aspect), Degen (2018, p. 1079) describes the 'conceived temporalities of urban planning' in terms of "rationally abstracted space and time which is mentally conceived of in verbal, visual or written representations and imaginaries". In the case of Belval, the juxtaposition of contemporary architecture and industrial heritage (thereby creating what Doel, 1996, would term 'disjointures'), so as to retain a sense of the history of the locale, is an important element of the masterplan. This is explicitly articulated in the documentation about the site:

> The key feature of the conversion project is the conservation and integration of elements of the old industrial site into a new urban sector... The Blast Furnaces and the industrial remains bear witness to an important part of history and become emblems of the new Belval. They offer a new public utility and host a mix of functions: learning and workplaces, public squares and neighbourhood amenities.
>
> (Le Fonds Belval, 2022.)

Thus, the blast furnaces at Belval could be regarded as huge 'disjointures'—where in this case, the present is in many ways constructed around the past (see Figure 6.2) in an attempt to secure the future of the area. Indeed, in 2022, Esch-sur-Alzette, was one of three cities to have the European Capital of Culture (ECC) designation; in part because of the aim "to celebrate the diversity and history of a cross-border region in the heart of Europe". Esch-sur-Alzette's ECC website implicitly acknowledges Ricoeur's (1984) notion of the 'threefold present' mentioned in earlier chapters, with its REMIX theme. An emphasis

Figure 6.2 Part of the City of Science development, from the roof of the blast furnaces, Belval, Luxembourg. Photograph by the author.

on temporality is clearly evident the Esch2022 website when articulating various aspects of the REMIX theme. For example, 'REMIX Culture' "includes all forms or artistic expression, but it also covers the numerous elements that define us as human beings. REMIX Culture means our history, our traditions, our geographical roots and the numerous aspects of our lives within this culture-rich region". Similarly, the 'REMIX Future' theme "aims to celebrate the diversity and history of a cross-border region in the heart of Europe. It tells the history of its evolution. What can the journey from the industrial era to the knowledge society tell us about its future potential in the digital revolution" (see https://esch2022.lu/en/get-to-know-e22/).

Considering the perceived space of Lefebvre's spatial triad, Degen (2018) considers the visible material aspects of the past (such as those manifested on such a huge scale in Belval) as 'perceived temporalities of the environment', which comprises "a temporal notion of the built environment as a malleable and recyclable construction that planners are in charge of" (ibid, p. 1083). In the specific context of this book, malleability and recyclability are inevitably linked to how both longstanding and new materialities can lend themselves to becoming stereotypical, and often intertextual and (re)stylized, contributory elements of the place assemblages that emerge through the graphic and written representation work of place marketing. In Belval, for example, promotional imagery highlights at one extreme the small detail of past materialities, such as close-up images of machinery in the blast furnaces, and at the other extreme aerial views of the site as a whole. On a larger scale, Warnaby and Medway (2008) demonstrate how this stereotyping occurs regularly with place marketing campaigns, notably those that involve content featuring 'iconic' buildings and landmarks, where the association between landmark and place is so strong that the two become synonymous in peoples' minds (such as the Eiffel Tower and Paris).

Turning to the more intangible unconscious realm of spatial routines, habits and practices—perhaps constituting Lefebre's 'lived space'—it can be argued that the movement of people and the flows of life (Anderson, 2012, p. 579) can create their own disjointures in the time-space continuum, thereby contributing to the notion of place as involving different levels of practice and performance (Cresswell and Hoskins, 2008). This accords with Degen's ideas about the 'lived temporalities of everyday life', which situate us "biographically within an environment", and also demonstrates how we might construct "a sense of place through regular interactions and uses" (2018, p. 1084). These interactions and uses might on the one hand involve routine, almost unthinking everyday activities for individuals, such as the students in the Science Faculty at the University of Luxembourg at Belval, routinely working in a modern library based somewhat incongruously within an old steel furnace (see Figure 6.3). On the other hand, these interactions may be communal and only occur occasionally, but nevertheless have great significance for those involved—such as religious processions through towns

Figure 6.3 Library, Belval. Photograph by the author.

and cities (which can serve a place-making function—see Platt and Medway, 2022). Such practices, in turn, may play an important role in place attachment and experience, and when sufficiently compelling, these discourses around routines and practices could potentially provide engaging place marketing narratives.

Linking back to the *perceived* within Lefebvre's spatial triad, there are invariably some material traces (however minor) that urban routines, habits and practices can leave behind, such as a popular route for pedestrians gradually worn into the paving stones of the city, or the slow temporal build-up of scratches along a bank of railings where commuters regularly lock their bikes. These 'materialized immaterialities' may have representational potential in place marketing/branding effort, particularly if they are supported by powerful memory discourses. For example, tourist visitors to Moscow are regularly directed towards the 76 bronze statues of Soviet citizens in Ploschad Revolutsii metro station. Here, attention is often drawn to the gleaming nose of a dog held by one of the figures, polished by millions of luck-seeking touches from passing Muscovites. This is a materialization of daily routines that features prominently on some of the city's tourism promotion websites (see for example, www.weheart.moscow/metro/).

Hence, I would concur with Anderson's (2012) contention that "it is more appropriate to think of place not as something formed by the assembly of stable component parts which are connected together but, rather, in terms of unstable entities/processes which converge" to bring about "a coming together of mutual interaction and interference" (ibid, p. 582)—perhaps evident of a kind of (to use Serres's term) *percolation*, which incorporates notions of both fluidity and fixity. Accordingly, place marketing representation work, too, incorporates aspects of both *fluidity* (inherent in the concept of relational places and the ongoing (re)assemblage efforts required to create place marketing narratives), and *fixity* (in that the 'essence' of the place will accrete over time, and the creation of a sense of attachment to place should be a key marketing and branding task).

The temporal implications of these notions of fluidity and fixity have some parallels with Bergson's (2002) concept of duration (*Durée*)—the key features of which are *multiplicity* and *continuity*. Bergson suggests that multiplicity can be both spatial and temporal, and can be accommodated both quantitatively (relating to, for example in this specific context, the number of different stakeholders that can be involved in place marketing), and qualitatively (relating to, in this context, the fact that these multiple stakeholders will have different perspectives, ethea and attitudes—some of which may relate to their perception of time and its importance/relevance—arising from their different identities). In his discussion of Bergson's work in the urban context, Madanipour notes that:

> The ontological multiplicity of the city combines both forms of Bergsonian multiplicity: the intensifying diversity of individualized humans and objects with which we live, which creates a spatial multiplicity, and the inherent and magnified diversity of our states of mind, which creates and magnifies temporal multiplicity.
>
> (2017, p. 83)

Resonating with aspects of the earlier discussion relating to differing perceptions of temporality (see for example, Reynolds et al., 2023), Madanipour (2017, p. 84) suggests that Bergson had an "observer-dependent sense of time", and in the context of the city, given that it is "the gathering place of thousands and millions of such observers, its temporality is therefore made of thousands or millions of durations and fluxes, simultaneous and discordant, all experienced alongside one another". The implications for how these temporal aspects of place marketing narratives are created—and, as discussed earlier, potentially contested—is a subject for more extensive and detailed future research, some avenues for which are sketched out below by way of conclusion.

A temporal research agenda for place marketing and branding

In understanding the relevance of temporality to place marketers—in terms of the most appropriate and constructive appropriation of history to achieve their objectives with regard to how the place is represented—one concept that has much utility is the notion of the *useable past*. Writing in the context of legal studies and from the standpoint of a constitutional lawyer, Sunstein describes the useable past as pointing to the goal of "finding elements in history that can be brought fruitfully to bear on current problems" (1995, p. 603). In the context of this book, designing and implementing effective place marketing and branding activities could be regarded as examples of 'current problems' that may, at least in part, be addressed by bringing a temporal perspective to bear on them—in other words, by incorporating certain aspects of the past into the marketing narrative of a place. In doing this, the historical past is potentially reinterpreted for contemporary use, consistent with the notion articulated by Hodgkin and Radstone (2003) that history is as much about the present as it is about the past. Inevitably—as discussed in in Chapter 2—this will be a selective process: some aspects of the past will be unusable as they do not fit with current place narrative(s) in that they are not deemed to be acceptable to a contemporary sensibility. Consequently are 'forgotten'—as discussed in Chapter 3.

Furthermore, and consistent with the view that place marketing activity is a social and political construction (Sadler, 1993), the choice of those aspects of a place's past that are deemed either 'usable' (and subsequently incorporated into place marketing representation work), or unusable (and consequently marginalized, or indeed, actively ignored as they are not consistent with 'official' narratives), can be contested. Hodgkin and Radstone state:

Our understanding of the past has strategic, political and ethical consequences. Contests over the meaning of the past are also contests over the meaning of the present and over ways of taking the past forward.

(2003, p. 1)

Hodgkin and Radstone (2003) go on to note that such contests are often not about what actually happened, but more about how the past is represented and who or what is entitled to speak for the past in the present—issues that are discussed in a specific place branding context by Reynolds et al. (2023). This may involve debates about the legitimacy of even appropriating the past for the purposes of place marketing and branding—and the qualifications of place marketers to be able to make judgements as to what is or is not included, particularly when the historical elements that are appropriated to this end are selective, with some voices marginalized or ignored. Thus, there is a danger that such appropriation becomes 'history-lite' and overly privileges just one—possibly contested—perspective of the past.

Indeed, the *processes* by which the choice of which history to use, and the implications for how the place is perceived (by residents and other internal stakeholders, as much as the external audiences that are the usual targets of such activities) is an area ripe for further, more detailed, investigation. Reynolds et al. (2023) identify how different stakeholders, depending on their perspective(s), may position a place differently in time. This in turn, could lead to tensions regarding how the place is represented externally in marketing and branding activities. Adopting an omni-temporal perspective (resonating with Ricoeur's, 1984, notion of the threefold present), Reynolds et al. state that whilst the heritage and history of a place seem will likely influence its branding in the present, there will be an "inevitable countervailing pull from an imagined future identity and aspirations about the sort of place its key stakeholders desire it to become" (2023, p. 9).

This links to another avenue for further research, in terms of more detailed investigation into *how* temporal dimensions are actually incorporated into place marketing messages. This book has outlined various examples of how temporal dimensions have been used in place marketing and branding activity, but more research is needed if the factors influencing the choice of elements from the past in current marketing/branding activities—and the practicalities of how this incorporation of the past is accomplished—are to be more fully understood. I hope that is book is a useful first step in this endeavour.

References

Anderson, J. (2012). Relational places: The surfed wave as assemblage and convergence. *Environment and Planning D: Society and Space*, 30: 570–587. http://dx.doi.org/10.1068/d17910

Bergson, H. (2002). *Key Writings*. London: Continuum.

Cresswell, T. (2004). *Place: A Short Introduction*. Malden MA/Oxford/Victoria: Blackwell Publishing.

Cresswell, T. and Hoskins, G. (2008). Place, persistence, and practice: Evaluating historical significance at Angel Island, San Francisco, and Maxwell Street, Chicago, *Annals of the Association of American Geographers*, 98(2): 392–413. https://doi.org/10.1080/00045600701879409

Crinson, M. and Tyrer, P. (2005). Clocking off in Ancoats: Time and remembrance in the post-industrial city. In M. Crinson (Ed.) *Urban Memory: History and Amnesia in the Modern City*. London and New York: Routledge, pp. 49–71.

Degen, M. (2018). Timescapes of urban change: The temporalities of regenerated streets. *The Sociological Review*, 66(5): 1074–1092. https://doi.org/10.1177/0038026118771290

Doel, M. A. (1996). A hundred thousand lines of flight: A machinic introduction to the nomad thought and scrumpled geography of Gilles Deleuze and Félix Guattari. *Environment and Planning D: Society and Space*, 14: 421–439. https://doi.org/10.1068/d140421

Doel, M. A. (1999). *Poststructuralist Geographies: The Diabolical Art of Spatial Science*. Edinburgh: Edinburgh University Press.

Historic England (2016). *Heritage Counts 2016 – Heritage and Place Branding*. Available at: https://historicengland.org.uk/content/heritage-counts/pub/2016/heritage-and-place-branding-pdf/ [Accessed 23 May 2019].

Hodgkin, K. and Radstone, S. (2003). Introduction: Contested pasts. In K. Hodgkin and S. Radstone (Eds.) *Contested Pasts: The Politics of Memory*. London and New York: Routledge, pp. 1–21.

Huyssen, A. (2003). *Present Past: Urban Palimpsests and the Politics of Memory*. Stanford: Stanford University Press.

Kalandides, A. (2011). The problem with spatial identity: Revisiting the "Sense of place". *Journal of Place Management and Development*, 4(1): 28–39. https://doi.org/10.1108/17538331111117142

Le Fonds Belval (2022). *Belval Exposition La Cité des Sciences*. Esch-sur-Alzette, Luxembourg: Le Fonds Belval.

Lefebvre, H. (1991). *The Production of Space* (trans. D. Nicholson-Smith). Oxford: Blackwell Publishing.

Madanipour, A. (2017). *Cities in Time: Temporary Urbanism and the Future of the City*. London: Bloomsbury Academic.

Platt, L. and Medway, D. (2022). Sometimes…Sometimes…Sometimes…Witnessing urban placemaking from the immanence of "the middle". *Space and Culture*, 25(1): 105–120. https://doi.org/10.1177/1206331219896261

Reynolds, L., Peattie, K., Koenig-Lewis, N. and Doering, H. (2023). There's a time and place: Navigating omni-temporality in the place branding process. *Journal of Business Research*, 170: 114308. http://dx.doi.org/10.1016/j.jbusres.2023.114308

Ricoeur, P. (1984) *Time and Narrative Volume 1* (trans. K. McLaughlin and D. Pellauer). Chicago and London: The University of Chicago Press.

Ross, D., Saxena, G., Correia, F. and Deutz, P. (2017). Archaeological tourism: A creative approach. *Annals of Tourism Research*, 67: 37–47. https://doi.org/10.1016/j.annals.2017.08.001

Sadler, D. (1993). Place marketing, competitive places and the construction of hegemony in Britain in the1980s. In G. Kearns and C. Philo (Eds.) *Selling Places: The City as Cultural Capital Past and Present*. Oxford: Pergamon Press, pp. 175–192.

Serres, M. with Latour, B. (1995). *Conversations on Science, Culture and Time* (trans R. Lapidus). Ann Arbor MI: University of Michigan Press.

Sunstein, C. R. (1995). The idea of a useable past. *Columbia Law Review*, 95: 601–608.

Warnaby, G. and Medway, D. (2008). Bridges, place representation and place creation. *Area* 40(4): 510–519. https://doi.org/10.1111/j.1475-4762.2008.00825.x

Index

Note: *Italicized* page references relate to the figures.

For Product Safety Concerns and Information please contact our EU
representative GPSR@taylorandfrancis.com
Taylor & Francis Verlag GmbH, Kaufingerstraße 24, 80331 München, Germany

www.ingramcontent.com/pod-product-compliance
Ingram Content Group UK Ltd.
Pitfield, Milton Keynes, MK11 3LW, UK
UKHW021822240425

457818UK00006B/36